SINGLE MOM AND THE CITY

SINGLE MOM AND THE CITY

CREATE TIME, MONEY, AND A RICH LIFE

TAKIYAH

EDITOR NIYAH LA'DON

SINGLE MOM AND THE CITY

Author Takiyah
Editor Niyah La'Don
Back cover photo by Zotunde Morton

Copyright Single Mom And The City 2020

ISBN: 978 0 578 75393 5

Published in the United States of America

This book is dedicated to my amazing parents, Isaiah and Hakima (Kemo) Smith. Without you, I would not be the me I am today. I am lucky to be a perfect combination of both of you. Rest in paradise. To my beautiful, brilliant, Niyah. Your love and support have been paramount. Your presence in my life is a blessing greater than I could have ever conceived. I sometimes find myself just staring at you, in awe of the wonderful human I brought into this world. Without you, there would be no *Single Mom And The City*.

Acknowledgments

Dearest Niyah, you are my inspiration, my motivation, and #1 cheerleader. Thank you for supporting me in innumerable ways, you cease to amaze me. You are a beautiful example this book will benefit moms and children. Without you, there would be no Single Mom And The City. My heart beats for you.

To my little brother Malik, you have been a blessing to our life. You are a true example of happiness and positivity. Thank you for your unconditional love.

A special thank you to my financial contributors:

- Ernie McNabb, a huge thank you, for your generous donation towards this book. Thank you for being so selfless with your time, and inspiring through words and actions. Your wonderful energy is infectious.
- Fred Wikkeling, Thank you for your continued support, words of wisdom, and opening my mind to new concepts that allow for even more abstract thinking.
- Shirley Baker, To my Aunt, my birthday triplet, my kindred spirit, I am blessed to be a part of your lineage.
- Janell N. Kelley, You are a fantastic example of someone who began with a dream, put in all of your efforts until you achieved. You are proof that anything is possible.
- Magdy (The Clothing Coach), your creativity is contagious. It's wonderful to have so many philosophical

commonalities. Thank you for your support, a true
gentleman.

- Odessa Omoroghomwan Weaver, thank you for your
  support and showing the world what a loving family
  looks like. A true inspiration.
- Deanna Omoroghomwan, you are a perfect example
  of having a dream and making it come true. You make
  motherhood look easy.

Carolyn Samiere, to go through life not knowing someone
but to meet years later and find out our paths crossed many,
many times. Life is interesting that way. Thank you for sharing
your journey.

Solana Paz, thank you for the many days spent brain-
storming at the coffee shop. You are a true example that it is
never too late to follow your dreams.

Kenneth Fax, thank you for the insight, and abundance
of ideas for Single Mom And The City. Thank you for sharing
your words of wisdom.

Barbara Rose Brooker, thank you for sharing your decades
of wisdom as a fellow author.

I would like to express my deepest gratitude and appreciation to everyone who has helped make this book a reality.
Whether it was through inspiration, words of encouragement
or being a sounding board. Thank you all.

Single Moms are angels that graced the earth as a blessing
to children. Mom's just make the world a better place. You are
incredible. Thank you for all that you do.

Contents

INTRODUCTION
WHAT DO YOU WANT?

"We can all be the best mom, yet it will always look different."

Takiyah

SINGLE MOM AND *The City* was created for the Mom who desires more than a life of mediocrity. This book is for the woman who is motivated to become the best version of herself and live a happy, fulfilled, successful life, while growing children into happy, healthy, fabulous little beings. Let's embark on this journey together.

There are more than ten million single moms in the United States alone. If I help even one Mom through knowledge gained over the years from education, research, and life's lessons compiled throughout the pages of this book, then it all would have been worth it.

The Foundation of Creation

Every great thing that has ever happened in this world began with a thought. So what do you want in life? What do you want out of life? We all have the ability to dream and create—the grander and more palatial the dream is, the better. What's most amazing about dreaming is that it's not necessary to know how it will be accomplished. There are just three requirements. 1.) Set your intentions, 2.) Have faith that it will happen, and 3.) Begin moving in the direction of your dream.

Consistency is the key to accomplishing goals. Ask yourself every single day: What can I do today, that my future self will thank me for? This puts things into perspective when you want a better life for yourself and your family. A fabulous life is created by small, simple routines we do every day and night. These rituals become our habits, and eventually our lifestyle.

"Nothing will work, unless you do."

Maya Angelou

Lights. Camera. Action!

Targeted Action

Is what you say you want, lining up with your daily actions?

From infancy, we talk and act like those around us. If English were the sole language spoken in the home, then that is what would be learned. If there were four additional languages spoken, we would learn those as well. We model and adapt to our environment. If one spends a large amount of time with those that are articulate, confident, intelligent, productive and successful, we begin to mimic those traits. Conversely, if you spend much of your time with those that watch television all day, drink alcohol excessively, curse incessantly and are always negative, you will too, begin to imitate those traits. We are often a reflection of what we see, hear, think, and do.

As you go about your daily life, be sure to ask yourself the following. Am I moving in the direction of my dreams, or am I moving further away from my dreams? Allow your answer to guide your actions. Ask and you shall receive. Seek, and you shall find. It's really as simple as that.

You will find that when you are moving in the direction of your dreams, blessings and opportunities will arise. If you are reading this book right now, it is not by coincidence. It's just the beginning of a positive, impactful change in your life. Opportunities, favorable circumstances, and people will begin to enter your life, to guide, support, and assist on your journey. You may also enter the life of someone you could be of service to, even if only for inspiration. In the world and in the universe, we are all connected and intertwined in some way. No one lives on an island alone; we all need human connection and assistance. Humans are the most evolved animals on the planet, complete with our infinite complexities. Our ability to create and achieve is unlimited.

Creation begins in the mind, next your belief system, followed by targeted action.

Mahatma Gandhi said, "The future depends on what you do today."

As you read this book, may each word bless you with health, happiness, and abundance beyond your wildest dreams.

With love and appreciation,
Single Mom And The City

CHAPTER ONE
CREATE THE LIFE YOU WANT

"Thoughts are the greatest vehicle to change, power and success in the world. Everything begins with thought."

Oprah Winfrey

DON'T TALK, ACT.

Don't say, SHOW.

Don't promise, PROVE.

7 Secrets to Creating the Life You Want.

1. **Believe in yourself.** You must believe in yourself, or no one else will. Motivation comes from within. Allow your children and ancestors to be the driving factors that propel you to greatness.

2. **Believe it is possible.** All throughout history the impossible has been made possible. Your dreams are no different.

3. **Be Positive and Optimistic.** Like attracts like. Our circumstances are often a reflection of our attitude, be it positive or negative. Bless your surroundings with your radiance and positive attitude. Your experiences are often a mirror image of what you project to the world.

4. **Expect the best, and you will attract the best.** People will treat you as well as you treat yourself. Never lower your standards or apologize for having them.

"Keep your standards and heels high."

~ Coco Chanel

5. **What you need, you will attract.** Be in alignment with what you want. You want to start a business. Have you begun researching? Are you attending networking events among people in your field of interest? Or are you watching reality television in your free time, or scrolling social media, watching other people live their best lives through a screen, instead of living your dream life? Ask yourself, "As I hang out with my friends who smoke and drink all day, will I be likely to hang out in elite circles and attend fancy events, like I said I wanted to do?" Most importantly, ask yourself, "Am I being the role model I want to be for my children? Am I setting a good example?"

"Whatever you consume, will consume you."

~ Ralph Smart

6. **Don't let your circumstances program you.** There is a very small percentage of people who grew up with a "perfect life". If we choose to remain in circumstances we are unhappy with; then we have only ourselves to blame. Create the life you want to live. The answers are at your fingertips, within this book.

7. **Take calculated chances.** There is so much growth outside of your comfort zone.

Beware of those who have failed or haven't accomplished their dreams. They will use the two words that should be stricken from the dictionary and erased from your vocabulary: "can't and impossible". The most successful people in the world have been told "you can't" or "it's impossible". Remember. Someone else's opinion doesn't make it true.

Keep your dreams and desires close to your heart.

It can be very tempting to want to shout your dreams/goals from the rooftop. It's super exciting! However, some may not understand why you have such goals. Everyone will not bask in your enthusiasm. Believe it or not, everyone will not have the best intentions for your desires toward wanting a better life. They may be vocally or silently spreading negative energy upon you—"friends" and "family" included. "Who does she think she is!" "She thinks she's better than us!" People will try to poke holes in your ideas, and tell you that it has never been done before, or say it's not realistic. It is not your job to get non-believers on board. Simply show them with your actions.

"Being realistic is the most common path to mediocrity."
Will Smith

What Research Says About Announcing Your Goals.

There is a common misconception that sharing your goals with the world helps you achieve them. However, the research shows otherwise. Let's say you are going to write a book! When you share this news with a friend, let's assume they congratulate you and tell you how amazing you are. As you describe in detail your vision, it causes an endorphin rush. You receive an emotional reward, a premature win! This tells your unconscious mind that it has already happened, which causes loss of motivation, making your goal more difficult to achieve.

Who can I share my goals/dreams with?

1. Journal
2. Mentor
3. Accountability Partner
4. Personal/Business Advisor
5. Cheerleader (an enthusiastic and vocal supporter: someone that openly wants to see you succeed)

7 Simple Action Steps to Take Now

1. **Guide your life in the direction you choose.** There are no do-overs in life. Get in the driver's seat and live the life that you want. Ask yourself, "What is the most effective and efficient use of my time now?"
2. **Write it down.** Write down a detailed description of exactly what you want.
3. **Speak it into existence.** Read it aloud three times a day; when you wake up, in the afternoon and right before you go to bed.
4. **Visualize.** If you can see it, you can be it. Envision yourself having obtained your wildest dreams. Feel the feelings and emotions as if you were experiencing and living what you are visualizing. Put imagery of your goals around your home. Keep a picture in your wallet or phone. We become what we think.
5. **Meditate and Pray.** Sit still in a quiet place and meditate and/or pray. Quiet your mind and focus on taking slow controlled deep breaths. Do this twice a day, preferably when you wake up in the morning and before you go to bed at night. Keep a notepad close by. Wonderful ideas tend to flow while sitting in silence alone.

6. **Act.** Do something every single day that will bring you closer to your dreams. Your cumulative actions will result in your outcome. Little things become big things.
7. **Learning is perpetual.** Read books. Attend workshops or classes and acquire additional knowledge and skills.

"I truly believe that if you put your goals in writing, speak them out loud, and work for them, they will happen."

Ciara

Fear versus Faith

- To believe in fear is to believe in something you cannot see.
- To believe and to have faith is to believe in something you cannot see.

It is more beneficial to choose Faith. Ultimately, you get to decide. Feel the fear, and do it anyway. Ask yourself. What would you do, if you knew you couldn't fail? What life would you create for yourself if you were guaranteed to be successful?

There is no magic lamp that will instantaneously grant your heart's desires. Your dreams will never work unless you do. Do little things in a great way, every day!

"The best way to predict the future is to create it."

Unknown.

CHAPTER TWO
THE POWER OF MEDITATION
TAP INTO YOUR INFINITE POSSIBILITIES.

*"The beauty of life does not reside in certainty or conformity.
It resides in the infinite possibilities of uncertainty."*

Debasish Mridha

Intuition

INTUITION IS YOUR superpower. It is the ability to know or understand something without conclusive evidence. It is an instinct or gentle nudge we feel when we are being guided in a certain direction. Women were born with intuition. Use it as a guide in life. Daily meditation allows you to be more in tune with your senses and intuition.

The Power of Sensory Meditation

What happens in the brain when practicing yoga and sensory meditation?

Sensory meditation focuses on being present and absorbing what is happening in the moment. This type of meditation uses one or more of the five senses which includes: listening to sounds, smelling aromas, staring softly, feeling with the body or hands, and tasting. It is important to acknowledge what our senses are absorbing, without judgment.

Assistant Professor of Psychology at Harvard Medical School, Sara Larza, conducted a study that compared the brain scans of people who have been meditating for years and those who have never meditated. What was found was an increase in gray matter in individuals that meditated. "Gray matter contains most of the brain's neuronal cell bodies. The gray matter includes regions of the brain involved in muscle control, and sensory perception such as seeing and hearing, memory, emotions, speech, decision making, and self-control." Studies have also shown a capacity for increased creativity and empathy while simultaneously decreasing stress and depression when individuals meditate. When people reported a decrease in stress there was a reduction in the amygdala. The primary function of the amygdala is memory, decision-making, and emotional responses such as fear, stress, and aggression. Science confirms that meditation reduces stress and increases sensory perception, which, in turn, when you meditate, you will be more in touch with your senses and intuition. Research has also shown that gray matter reduces in pregnancy and can last for at least two years after birth. Hence the term, "Mommy Brain."

4 Common Forms of Meditation

1. **Guided Meditation:** One is guided through the meditation process via video, voice recording or in-person instruction. This form of meditation consists of verbal instruction and/ or music.
2. **Mantra Meditation:** A favorite phrase or prayer is repeated quietly while concentrating on your words and breath.
3. **Mindfulness Meditation:** A mental training that practices living in the present moment. This practice focuses on

breath flow, body awareness, mental images, mind, and body relaxation.

4. **Yoga:** Yoga, which is defined as a union, is a perfect balance. It is the harmony of the physical through exercise, combined with meditation and peace.

Meditation is one of the few exercises that feed the mind, body, and soul simultaneously. It is extremely easy to begin and takes up little time and provides substantial rewards. A great time to meditate is when you first wake up and before you go to sleep. The reason why morning meditation or prayer is so important is because you are setting your intentions and feeding your mind after the rejuvenation period. Nighttime meditation or prayer is equally important because you are telling your subconscious what to think and dream about while your body rejuvenates during sleep. Whether you choose to nourish your mind with positivity or feed it poison is entirely up to you.

If you are new to meditation, practice in five-minute increments and increase as your endurance builds. Forty minutes a day will provide maximum benefits. Guided meditation can be easiest to begin with, because a soothing voice walks you through every single step. Try all forms of meditation until you determine which works best for you. YouTube has a ton of free videos for all meditation forms. Teach your children how to meditate as well. In a world of social media and busy lives, children can also benefit from meditation.

Customize It.

Once you get familiar with meditation, customize it to meet your needs perfectly. Combine information and techniques that you enjoy. Record your voice with your exact specifications. Speak your dreams in the present tense.

13

I enjoy listening to my recording while I am lying in bed in the mornings and at night. It's a great way to include meditation into your mornings if you are short on time. Insert your dreams and goals into your recording. Be as detailed as possible. Some examples are: "I am happy. I am healthy. I am an amazing Mom. I am financially abundant; my new business is thriving etc." Ninety percent of the time, I fall asleep before my recording ends. The information permeates your unconscious mind while you sleep. This is why it is important to feed your brain with positive information. As your body is regenerating for the upcoming day, your mind is working, and your unconscious mind is being programmed. You can literally choose your state of mind to aid in programming your actions.

Create a recording for your children as well. I have made recordings for my daughter filled with specific dialogue such as, "I am" statements and other positive, confidence-boosting words. Feel free to throw in, "I will make my bed," and "I will always treat my Mom with love and kindness." I definitely did. I am always sure to speak love into the recordings such as, "You are healthy, intelligent, and beautiful inside and out. You are loved and blessed beyond measure."

It is extremely important that you always keep the words you use positive. Why? Whether you realize it or not, words are extremely powerful and affect the subconscious mind. Instead of saying, "I hope I don't run into traffic. I hope I'm not late for my job interview. I hope I don't lose my job," you would alternately say, "I am early and prepared for my job interview. I will be on time and relaxed for my job interview. My bank account is thriving and many employers want to hire me."

Meditation provides infinite benefit to the mind, body, and soul. Moms and children reap the rewards of a more relaxed you. I highly recommend teaching your children to meditate as well. When the mind is clear, there is room for dreaming and creating. Science agrees that meditation has a positive impact on our minds by allowing for better decision-making while reducing stress. High stress is a reality for many single moms. So, take a moment in your day to pour back into yourself.

Meditate. Rejuvenate. Create.

"Whatever we plant into our subconscious mind and nourish with repetition and emotion will one day become a reality."

Earl Nightingale

CHAPTER THREE
THE 80/20 RULE

*"Hack away all the unessential . . . the height of culti-
vation always runs on simplicity. I always believe that the
easy way is the right way."*

Bruce Lee

IN MOST AREAS of life, 80 percent of the results will come from
20 percent of the actions. Thus, it is more important to focus
on the 20 percent that will produce the largest impact. Having
an 80/20 frame of mind, helps keep you focused, and improves
outcomes.

How the 80/20 Rule came to be:

The concept behind the 80/20 rule came from Vilfredo
Pareto. He first noticed that 20 percent of the pea plants in
his garden grew 80 percent of the healthy pea pods. Pareto
further observed that approximately 80 percent of Italy's land
was owned by 20 percent of the population. He later surveyed
other countries and discovered the dispersion was similar.

Additional Data

- In 1988, many video rental shops reported that 80 percent of the revenue came from 20 percent of the videotapes.
- Microsoft has learned that by repairing the top 20 percent of the largest reported bugs, 80 percent of the relevant errors and crashes would be eradicated.
- If we compared the 80/20 Rule with the NBA, this rule holds true. There is a small percentage of players who provide substantial contributions in terms of points, rebounds, defense/steals, etc., which has a sizable impact on the team's win.
- Eighty percent of businesses' profits come from 20 percent of their customers.

The rule continues to hold true in our household. We eat 20 percent of the food in our refrigerator 80 percent of the time. When I think about the shoe collection I once owned (over 100 pairs), I only wore about twenty to twenty-five pairs. I have since downsized to about twenty-five pairs which include sandals, boots, casual, athletic, and dress shoes. Interestingly, the 80/20 rule still holds true, even with the downsize. I wear five to six pairs of my collection most. The same holds true with clothing. Most people only wear about 20 percent of their wardrobe on a regular basis. How about you?

80/20 Rule and Children

When children like you, they are more likely to cooperate. They will aim to please you, listen, and be accepting of morals and lessons. Only 20 percent of your interactions with children should be negative, and the remaining 80 percent should be positive. Of the 20 percent, it will include all directives such as criticisms, any negative comments, yelling, punishment, etc. – "anything" negative. Positive acts are loving on and building up your child. This includes giving compliments, praise, encouragement, playing a game, etc. Here is a super simple way to remember. Positivity would be any interaction that makes your child feel good: A cute nickname, hug, compliment, playing, or singing together. Negativity would be the opposite, where your child does not feel good: ignoring, anger, annoyance, lecturing, correction, etc.

We know how much we love our children; however, we must ensure that it shines through in our parenting and interactions. Much of parental communication can be compiled with threats and instruction, which can cause a child to feel unloved. Incorporating the 80/20 Rule into parenting creates a healthy foundation for positive parenting.

The 80/20 Rule is paramount in creating time, money, and a rich life. Focus on a small number of things because they have the potential to give you the greatest return on your investment in time, money, and results in general. This applies to work, health, exercise, relationships, and parenting. Have you ever found yourself continuously busy, without much to show for your effort? Implement the 80/20 rule and watch your productivity soar.

"If I can create a minimum of my plans and desires, there shall be no regrets."

Bessie Coleman

CHAPTER FOUR
OUTSOURCE, OUTSOURCE, OUTSOURCE IT ALL!

"Outsourcing equals freedom."

Takiyah

DO YOU LOVE scrubbing toilets? Are you thrilled to find the sink full of dishes because you get the pleasure of washing them? Do you jump for joy when the laundry is full because you are now blessed to wash/dry and fold? If you answered no to one or more of the questions listed above, then this chapter is for you!

Welcome to the world of outsourcing! Some may find this concept foreign. However, most of us outsource tasks on a daily basis and don't even realize it. Have you ever purchased a coffee, tea, or smoothie from your local barista? Had a pizza delivered (or picked up)? Purchased a bagged meal from a grocery store that you simply had to heat in a pan or microwave? Have you taken pants to the cleaners to be hemmed or have a button sewn on a blouse? Called a rideshare to take you to an event because you didn't want to drive? Any time you pay someone to perform a task that you can do yourself, you are outsourcing.

Outsourcing mundane tasks that do not bring you joy while performing said task is one of the biggest time-saving, happiness secrets of the successful single mom. I know what you're thinking. With outsourcing comes an additional cost. I could simply do it myself and use that money for something else? True. Convenience does come at a cost. Start small. Outsource the task that will have the most impact.

Can I afford to outsource?

Can you afford not too? Time goes by so fast as we grow older. Our little babies become toddlers, elementary students, then high school, next college. You will never get those precious moments back, and they truly go by in the blink of an eye. Just ask anyone with high school, college, or adult children. When your children are off at college, will you look back when they were younger and think, "Wow I scrubbed that toilet really well?" or will your narrative be, "I am so happy I outsourced some or all of the house chores to be able to spend more quality time with my kids, playing games, dancing, acting silly, and playing at the park?" Take the opportunity to build close, meaningful relationships with your little ones. You will thank yourself later.

Is cost a major factor?

Start by asking the father for additional monthly money (if you have contact with the father, of course). You have nothing to lose and everything to gain! Be honest. Inform him that you are experiencing additional stress and are unable to spend the quality time with your child that they deserve because you are busy doing A, B, and C. Dad has a vested interest in the child's well-being as well, so you may be surprised at the outcome.

Do your research before you have the conversation. Know the chores you want to outsource and the amount of the total cost. Estimate the additional time it would free up for you to spend with the child. Most importantly, approach the situation humbly and ask nicely. Remember the saying, you catch more bees with honey than you do with vinegar. It works. I asked for a contribution toward publishing this book from my ex, and I got it!

Work additional hours. The second easiest way to afford outsourcing would be to work additional hours to cover costs. This could be achieved by working as little as an additional hour per week, more or less, depending on your pay. Determine what additional amount you need to cover the outsourced task, and work the amount of hours accordingly. Ask yourself this question. Would you rather spend an additional "x" amount of hours on your job to pay to have your home cleaned, or would you rather clean it yourself?

It's okay to start small.

It's not necessary to outsource everything all at once. Unless, of course, it makes financial sense for you and your family.

Outsourcing may be a huge leap for some. So, begin in a way that feels good for you...and your budget. Try starting with laundry, especially if you have to go to the laundromat to wash and dry clothing. Many local laundry facilities and dry cleaners, wash, and fold clothing. Charges are typically calculated by the pound. Some laundry services will even pick-up, wash, and deliver your clean, folded laundry back to your doorstep. Now that's service! For the purpose of this book, I googled a dry cleaner that offers laundry service in San Francisco that has 211, four and a half out of five-star reviews. Note: If you can get a personal referral from someone you know, do so. Otherwise, check ratings/reviews. Their cost is $1.40 per pound, with a minimum of 10 pounds. This means you can spend as little as $14 dollars to have 10 pounds of laundry cleaned for you. Now that's magical!

Additionally, think about the cost of your detergent, the cost of the water, and the energy you are using if you wash at home. If you travel to the laundromat to wash, the cost you are spending on the machines and the agony of lugging all of that laundry to and from your home. Oh! And are you bringing the kids? Not so magical. . .We didn't even factor in your time. What is that worth? Hopefully, outsourcing is beginning to sound pretty good.

What can I outsource in my life that will make a huge impact?

Here is a list of potential tasks you can outsource. If there are things on this list you love doing, keep doing it! The goal is to spend the most time on things that bring you joy, like spending quality time with your children.

1. **Grocery delivery or curbside pick-up (curbside pick-up is often free).**

    Cost: Free - $100/year or $8.33/month

    Many stores offer free curbside pick-up, including big-box retailers like Target and Walgreens. You simply place your order online. Some stores can even have your order ready in as little as one hour. Think of how much time and money you will save if you aren't forced to shop aisle by aisle with kids. Whenever I go grocery shopping, I ALWAYS buy things that are not on my list. Choose to pay a little more and have groceries delivered directly to your home. There are businesses that offer pickup and delivery in as little as two hours. You can also schedule a day and time in the future. You could literally eliminate eating out if you wanted. Think of how much you would be saving. Tip: If these suggestions are not an option, and you shop with your child/children, consider allocating them a small shopping budget. I typically give $5 for one child. If you have multiple little ones, you can have them work as a team and choose a single item for a specified amount. Otherwise, they will want to put everything in the cart. You can instruct them that their choice needs to be healthy or semi-healthy (no candy). This is what I do. This tip gives your child a sense of inclusion, a concept of money, and working within a budget while understanding healthy food choices. Win. Win.

2. Meal delivery services

Cost: Approximately $30 - $100 per week (prices vary based on the number of servings and number of meals per week.)

Pre-measured, pre-packaged ingredients with recipes delivered to your doorstep. There are so many options of meal delivery services to choose from. I have found huge benefits from this service. My preference is two to three meals delivered per week. The rest of the time, I can choose from a few of my tried and tested favorites. The best thing about meal delivery services is that it enables you to try new dishes with new cooking techniques, which you can incorporate into your everyday cooking regimen. Include your children to help prepare meals. Suspend your membership at any time and resume when you are ready. If you love leftovers, the only downfall is that there won't be enough because you receive one serving per person. If you decide to try this service, find a coupon online. All of the services I have used offer a discount code for first-time customers. Definitely, worth the try even if you decide to cancel after the first week.

3. House cleaner/maid services

Cost: Varies widely depending on your area.

House cleaning is my most dreaded chore. Especially cleaning the kitchen/doing dishes and cleaning the toilet. Ick! I found myself ordering out several times throughout the week because the sink and countertops were piled with dishes. Sound familiar? I just could not cook with that kind of situation going on. When I calculated the amount of money I spent eating out, it only made sense to have a cleaning service come in. This truly is win, win all around. The money I was spending eating out is now going toward house cleaning service. My home stays overall tidy because I am able to maintain it until the cleaners come again (every other week). Also, we are eating healthier meals because I am cooking. Bonus. I am more zen and relaxed with a greater ability to create because my space is clean and relatively clutter-free. This outsourcing was the most beneficial, time-saving, smartest move I have made. My only wish is that I had done it sooner.

4. Laundry wash and fold

Cost: $1 - $3 per pound.

Laundry services are very reasonable, especially if you don't have an in-home washer/dryer. For babies or little children, this service can be particularly beneficial because their clothing is tiny with many pieces that don't weigh much (but can be time-consuming to sort and fold).

5. Interior Decorating

Cost: $60 and up per room. Hourly rates are typically available.

Do you want your home to be aesthetically pleasing and beautiful, but you don't want to do all of the work required? Nowadays, interior designers are available to help you online. I found that I am a little too detailed-oriented for the task of making my home beautiful. Interior design is something I later discovered I should have outsourced as I personally spent hours upon hours searching for inspiration rooms online, watching YouTube videos, researching countless retail sites, and in-store shopping. Then I spent several more hours scouring through websites' endless inventory of rugs to find the one that was just right. In short, the entire process took way too long (well over forty hours over the course of several months). My time would have been much better spent with my family or making more money and leaving the interior design to the experts. Note: Your interior does not need to be expensive in order to be aesthetically pleasing. I have been fortunate to find some items secondhand or heavily discounted. Having a clean, clear space just feels good and reduces stress. When our spaces are chaotic, we tend to feel stress. A clean and tidy space relaxes your mind and allows mental space for creation.

6. Task Rabbit

Cost: Varies (one-hour minimum)

Task Rabbit offers a variety of services like mounting and installation, moving and packing, furniture assembly, general handy-person services, errands, and more. This service is also extremely useful if you're in a last-minute pinch and need assistance immediately. Choose same day or future appointments. For me, building furniture can be a laborious, tedious task.

Outsourcing saves me the time and agony of a chore I don't enjoy. Also, hiring outside help for moving was the best thing I could have ever done. Let's face it, moving is not fun, and friends and family don't want to do it but they do because they care about us. Moving pretty much sucks. Hire someone, and have a friend oversee the movers and give direction—the other amazing benefit of hiring a moving company. Moving companies have insurance, so if they damage your precious belongings, you're covered. When friends damage your stuff, you're simply out of luck because you chose free, uninsured labor.

FYI: I looked online for a moving company and did not use task rabbit for that particular service.

7. Online Shopping:

This is a huge time and money saver. You can order just about anything online from the comfort of your own home and have it delivered to your doorstep for free or a low cost. I order everything from gifts, valentines treats, clothes, shoes, cleaning supplies, hygiene products, everything. . . When I buy items in-store, especially clothing or gifts, I almost always end up making impulse buys, thus spending more money. Online, impulse buys are greatly reduced because you can search exactly what you need, and if you end up with additional items in your cart, you can save, and think about if you really want it for a few days, thus greatly reducing buyer's remorse.

8. USPS Free Package Pickup:

Simply go online, pay, and schedule a pickup. The post office will pick up your pre-paid package for free. Complete online returns in a snap. What a time saver!

Outside of the US? Check your local mailing services to see if they offer similar services.

9. Transportation for kids to/from school and activities

Cost: Varies

There are lots of new companies in my area that now offer rides for minors. I have not personally used this service; however, I have friends who have found it extremely useful. The service can be used for taking your child to school, returning them home, sporting practices, activities, etc. Based on my own research, the criteria for drivers is stricter than the ones for ride-share companies that transport adults. Driving speed is monitored and they are required to adhere to the speed guidelines.

10. Birthday Parties

Cost: $200 and up

Who would have thought that outsourcing a birthday party could be so much fun and rewarding? Me! I had no idea, and I found out the hard way.

My daughter was three years old, and my help stood me up at the last minute!! I remember it like it was yesterday. The person shall remain nameless because it's water under the bridge at this point. Needless to say, I was throwing a party at an outdoor Funland. It was one-night prior. I needed to make food, arrive early to reserve the space then bring decorations, food and party bags, etc. to said location in the park. I was left to do all of this alone. Alone! I was tired, stressed, frustrated, and I vowed never to be in that situation again. Lesson learned.

The next birthday party was at an indoor Funland where all my guests and I had to do was show up. Oh! I brought the cake. That's it! It cost me about $300. Food, fun, and clean up, all-inclusive. I was able to enjoy my daughter and my guests. The other great thing is that as children get older, you can do children-only parties, which are even more cost-effective.

As I overcame my party planning jitters, several years later, I took a more active role in the planning process for an indoor/ outdoor party. However, I still outsourced some parts of the event. Planning ahead is key. Waiting until the last-minute breeds stress and panic. I made some of the food, and ordered the rest. I enlisted reliable close friends to lend a hand, and I hired entertainment to keep the children occupied so that I could still be able to enjoy my family and friends and merely oversee the party. Being a workhorse at your own party is not fun. Think of it this way; you spend time and money in making the day special; you're entitled to look back on the memories fondly and know that you also had a good time.

If you are thinking, I can't afford to spend $300 on a party, I'll do it myself. Think about all of the things you'll have to buy for the party, some that you may not use again. Costs add up quickly, while you're attempting to throw a cost-effective birthday without breaking the bank. I won't even get into the planning time, shopping time, etc. It equates to time and energy. Determine where you would like to spend yours— enjoying the party? Or working the party?

11. Automatic Bill-Pay

Cost: Free

Pay bills on a date designated by you, through your bank. Paying bills is probably one of the least desirable things to do. Money comes in, then "Poof!" it's gone. Taking this off of your plate of focus will be a huge relief. Automating your bills not only saves time but it creates mental space for something more desirable. Set aside about ten minutes per week to review your account. This gives you an opportunity to make sure all debits are valid and to check your balances.

Here's a true story. Approximately $127 was being taken electronically from my checking account monthly for over five years. I thought it was one of my student loan payments. Instead, I found out it was a motorcycle insurance payment for a bike I no longer owned! Mortified by this situation I called the insurance company to let them know I sold my motorcycle years ago. Once, I was able to speak to a representative, I explained what happened. Please note, I was super nice when I called. Being extremely courteous and polite always helps when you are asking for something. The lady on the phone apologized to me and asked that I send over proof of when the motorcycle was sold. Tadaaa!!! I received a check in the mail for approximately $7500.

Start small. It's not necessary to outsource everything all at once. Unless of course it makes financial sense for you and your family. Most of the suggestions I listed offer free or discounted prices the first time you try out the service. As the Super Mom that you are, think of outsourcing as your sidekick. Get help where it's most useful to you. Outsourcing equals more quality time with your children and more time for you.

Tip: When you are a first-time customer at any retailer or service business, always ask for a discount, stores usually offer one. Simply ask, "Are there any specials for new customers." You will be surprised by the additional savings you could benefit from.

"It's difficult to get things done, when there is no one to do it for you."

Takiyah

CHAPTER FIVE
PLEASING PERSONALITY
YOUR MOST POWERFUL ASSET.

"The greatest discovery of all time is that a person can change their future by merely changing their attitude."

Oprah Winfrey

PLEASING PERSONALITY: AN attractive personality; a personality that attracts.

Personality is the sum total of one's characteristics, appearances, mental, spiritual, and physical traits and habits that distinguish you from all others.

Your personality can be your greatest asset or liability. You get to decide.

Personality is representative of what cannot be seen, your character. However, people form their first impressions by outward appearances: your clothing, style of dress, hair, and makeup.

Life magically becomes easier with the cooperation and assistance of others. No one is living on an island; we all need each other in this lifetime. As a single mom, it is virtually impossible to live a fulfilled abundant life with zero assistance from others. Thus, a pleasing personality is valuable in all aspects of life: career, relationships, building networks, family, school, virtually any area that has dealings with people.

Be the kind of person everyone wants to be around, and you will have succeeded in having a pleasing personality. It begins with having a positive mental attitude. Your personality is like your signature, one of a kind. It can be molded into whatever you choose.

Three key traits of an attractive personality are:

• Smile
• Facial Expression
• Tone of Voice

Start with these three traits alone, and you are sure to improve every situation.

Think about people you enjoy being around, or that one person you know who brings light into every room they enter. They engage in conversation effortlessly, and people tend to gravitate toward them. Ever wondered what they have that you don't? Take a look at the list of the traits of a pleasing personality and see how many you already possess. Next, commit to practicing one or more new ones per week until you have adopted them all.

With change and improvement comes some discomfort. Just know that the changes you are implementing are for the greater good of yourself and children. Observe the positive changes you see in yourself and interactions with others. These positive changes in your "signature" will have a contagious effect on your children and generations to come.

"We can do anything we want to if we stick to it long enough."

Helen Keller

Pleasing Personality Traits

1. **Positive Mental Attitude (PMA):** This philosophy affirms that maintaining an optimistic temperament in every single situation in life attracts positive changes and elevates achievement. It can be achieved by having a confident, constructive, practical and positive mind no matter what the circumstances are.

2. **Flexibility of Mind:** The ability to understand and sympathize with other's points of view or way of doing things and to adapt in a way that creates harmony. This does not mean that you need to abandon your own view and "go with the flow" of someone else's ideas and thoughts. Those are spineless tendencies that are not recommended. Flexibility of mind is simply being able to harmonize ideas that cultivate the collaboration of attitudes and customs of others in such a way that creates and promotes a pleasant, successful, working relationship that is enjoyable. In other words, let go of a rigid mindset.

3. **Sincerity of Purpose:** Sincerity permeates through every word spoken, into every action and deed, and reflects itself in your thoughts so that even the most inexperienced at character analysis can recognize sincerity. Sincerity is the one trait/attribute through which the confidence of others is gained. Without it, you will be unlikely to gain true popularity and favorability. Your sincerity will reward you liberally in ways you may never have imagined. Remember, sincerity starts from within.

4. **Promptness of Decision:** This is a well-known trait in all successful people. Promptness of decision evolves as a result

of a self-confident, constructive, definitive, and increasing positive mental attitude. Has an idea or invention ever come to you that you did not act on? Then, at some later point in time someone acted on what you had once considered? Opportunity waits for no one. Definiteness of purpose is the starting point of all achievement.

5. **Common Courtesy:** Respecting people's rights and feelings in all situations. It is the habit of going out of your way to help someone less fortunate than yourself. Essentially, doing things for others without expecting direct compensation or reward. You must also control greed, jealousy, hatred, and selfishness. "Someone has said that courtesy is the cheapest yet the most profitable, of all traits of a pleasing personality."

6. **Tactfulness:** Tactfulness or having tact is a perceptive awareness of what to do or say in order to maintain good relationships and avoid language that may offend.

Beware of these actions that lack tactfulness:

a. Carelessness of tone: tone of voice can relay irritation, a negative attitude, and annoyance.

b. Cutting the speaker off while they are speaking.

c. Overuse of the word "I".

d. Inserting intimate or personal topics into the conversation whereby doing so can cause embarrassment to others.

e. Going to a place you have not been invited.

f. Pretentious and boastful. Over-praising of oneself represents inadequacy and weakness. Quite frankly, people are annoyed by it. Talent and ability need no introduction. You have never heard Michael Jordan say he is the greatest basketball player of all time. But, somehow everyone knows.

g. Calling people at cumbersome hours with no prior notice or consent.

h. Keeping people on the phone with pointless conversation.

i. Offering an opinion that no one asked for, particularly on subjects which you are not familiar with.

j. Disputing others' opinions.

k. Refusing others requests with an, "I'm too good for that" attitude.

l. Speaking to other people in a way that alludes you are better than them.

m. Correcting coworkers or employees in the presence of others.

n. Profanity and language that may offend.

o. Declaring what you dislike too openly.

p. Complaining about one's own physical ailments and adversity. Typically, the only people who are interested in this information would be lawyers, doctors, priests or other professionals who specialize in such a profession that requires them to help people out with specific challenges.

q. Criticizing or judging religious beliefs.

r. Entertaining malicious gossip.

s. Instead of "applauding" and building people up, one instead minimizes their personal achievements.

I was once blindly unaware what great impact tact has on those around us. Do you say and do the right thing at the right time? Oh, what a massive difference implementing tact had in my interactions with people.

7. **Pleasing Tone of Voice:** We express ourselves more through speaking than any other way. The voice is, more often than not, more expressive of true feelings of the speaker then the words itself. Voice tone is imperative and must be controlled so that the listener is pleased by the sound, and the words convey the intended message. For example, an irritated voice tone can dismantle a well-articulated sentence or paragraph.

8. **Facial Expression and the Habit of Smiling:** These two traits are closely related to voice control and smiling while speaking. People attempt to determine what is going on in the minds of others by observing their facial expressions, whether consciously or unconsciously. Think of the "poker face." A good poker player keeps their face neutral, unless in an attempt to lead or bluff the competition into thinking they have a great hand or bad hand. In either case, they change facial expressions as a reflection of what they are attempting to project. This trait is simple, yet powerful and impactful. Try smiling for twenty seconds and notice how your mood improves. Smile at someone who is frowning while saying hello, and observe their change in disposition.

9. **Tolerance:** The ability to be impartial and fair when opinions and belief systems differ from your own. Tolerance is simply keeping an open mind. One who is tolerant will remain open to receiving new and different information on all subjects. It is not necessary to take the information as facts. Examine and attempt to understand prior to reaching a just conclusion.

10. **Frankness in Manner and Speech:** Individuals of sound character and pleasing personality always have the courage to deal openly and directly with others. They are absolutely frank when they speak. Keep in mind, this frankness must be combined with courtesy, tact, and tolerance. Frankness

in manner and speech are indicative of sincerity. There is no substitute for sincerity.

11. **Keen Sense of Humor:** "Laugh and the world laughs with you; weep and you weep alone. . ." The intent is not to become a clown, unless it is your form of employment. However, a sense of humor that is well-developed helps individuals become at ease and grow warm. This trait will attract many people to you. A keen sense of humor has its own special kind of magic, which, when correctly mixed with tact, tolerance, courtesy, and sincerity will develop an attractive personality and will have a clear influence in acquiring popularity.

12. **Faith in Infinite Intelligence:** Infinite intelligence is a neutral term that applies to all faiths. Faith and belief must be included into every area of personal achievement. The intangible power of faith is the nucleus for all dreams, goals, and ultimately achievement.

13. **A Keen Sense of Justice:** Honesty that is deliberate and is the result of a helpful, wholesome, positive mental attitude. Justice in this sense, should not be altered or stretched to fit a particular circumstance or personal interest. A keen sense of justice is the standard, and your righteousness will motivate others to do what is right.

14. **The Appropriate Use of Words:** As human beings we have the capability to speak in words and enunciate distinctly. Choosing proper wording while speaking is key. The intent is to attract, not repel, so there is no excuse for offensive language. Profanity should be avoided. The dictionary has nearly 200,000 words for free use to articulate ourselves. I find it brilliant when an individual can produce a verbal thrashing to effectively get one's point across specifically and succinctly in the most polite manner. It makes it very difficult for the receiver to have a harsh rebuttal yet the

point is clear. The proper use of words can take you very far.

15. **Effective Speech:** Several aspects of pleasing personality must be combined in order to achieve effective speech. a.) Attractive and motivating voice tone. b.) Appropriate use of words. c.) Delivery and d.) Pleasant and active facial expressions. People who rise to great heights of personal achievement have the ability to sell ideas and themselves through effective speech.

16. **Control of Emotions:** Most people are ruled by their emotions. The good news is that we all have a choice. We can choose to control our emotions, and with this choice comes great power. Control can be accomplished by using self-discipline.

17. **Alertness of Interest:** Displaying attentiveness and active interest in the person one is engaging. People generally love to talk about themselves. It is an accomplishment and skill to actively listen while someone is speaking. Another amazing benefit of an alert mind is the ability to be aware and take advantage of opportunities when they present themselves.

18. **Versatility:** Having adaptable and versatile interest in subject-matter and people is essential to a pleasing personality. The person who knows little of anything outside of their own employment and personal affairs will be pleasing only to themselves. Individuals who are more popular are versatile and have at the very least a general knowledge of various subjects. Versatility enables one to understand people better. A versatile mind continually grows throughout life.

19. **Fondness for people:** Humans have an innate sense and can recognize when individuals like other people. We are

attracted to others who like people and are repelled by those that do not.

20. **Control of Temper:** Temper is an emotion of anger with free rein. An uncontrolled sharp tongue can destroy opportunities and the ability to be liked by people. However, this intense emotion will serve you well in personal achievement. The key is to control your temper rather than allow your temper to control you.

21. **Hope and Ambition:** Hope and ambition give life and drive to those that have it. Perseverance against odds is an attractive characteristic that others find appealing and worthy of imitation. People are attracted to this type of person in hopes that some of the fire that inspires and motivates them may rub off. People that continually strive for success are attracted to winners. We emulate and are often a reflection of who we surround ourselves with. You are the average of the five people you spend the most time with; they shape who you are. Tony Robbins, Jim Rhon and Tim Ferris believe in this rule.

22. **Temperance:** Temperance is moderation and self-restraint in all things, such as action, speaking, etc. One must have self-control and manage personal habits in order to have a pleasing personality. This especially includes eating, drinking, and sexual relations. Think temperance in all things and over-indulgence in nothing.

23. **Patience:** Patience is the quality of maintaining one›s composure and remaining calm while under any sort of distress such as pain, annoyance, misfortune, irritation etc. Patience is a form of discipline and essential in human relationships. Healthy personal habits aid in promoting patience, such as proper sleep/rest, exercise and a healthy diet. It can be much more difficult to have patience if one lacks adequate rest. The patient individual is one who

can maintain a mental attitude that is calm, confident, constructive, and wholesome. Patience truly is a virtue.

24. **Humility of Heart:** Humility of heart is an amazing trait. It describes someone that is on good terms with one's own conscience and in harmony with the creator. No matter how great the personal achievement or wealth one has amassed, it is important to remain grounded and humble.

25. **Appropriateness of Dress:** The best-dressed person is someone whose clothes fit well and flatter body type, color combinations compliment skin tone, and the outfit reflects personality and the occasion. If you want the best, aim for the best. You wouldn't wear a suit to play tennis, so why wear workout gear to work, unless you work at a gym. Imagine running into your ex and his new fiancée. How would you want to look? Always leave the house looking your best. You never know who you may run into or what opportunities may present themselves. No curlers or bonnets ever! Clothing does not make the person. However, it gives a favorable introduction. When you look good, you feel good and this gives off an air of self-confidence.

26. **Effective Showmanship/Show-womanship:** Effective show-womanship in this case is a winning personality combination pack of pleasing personality traits which include facial expression, control of voice tone, appropriate dress, proper choice of words, mastery of the emotions, courtesy, effective speech, versatility, a positive mental attitude, keen sense of humor, alertness of interest in other people and tactfulness. Quite the combo! The key to effective show-womanship is being able to dramatize circumstances and situations without offense to other people. Master this trait, and it will often pay off big when applied at the appropriate time.

27. **Clean Sportsmanship/Sportswomanship:** The individual that can win without bragging and lose without sulking and

complaining is someone who is likely to be popular among their peers. This person is known as a good sport. Habits learned in sports often become a part of one's character and can be of great benefit in all aspects of life. Poor sportswomanship is usually the result of some sort of insecurity.

28. **The Ability to Shake Hands Properly:** The proper handshake is coordinated with words of greeting, usually emphasizing every word with a firm grip of the hand. The hand is released once the spoken greeting is complete. Remember this is not a contest, and the objective is not to squeeze with all your might. The art of the handshake is important. An effective hand-shake conveys sincere emotion such as enthusiasm, fellowship, and liveliness.

29. **Personal Magnetism:** Personal magnetism is sex emotion. It is a personal attractiveness or charisma that enables you to influence others. As a woman and feminine being, this trait is extremely useful but should be controlled. This trait has priceless value, and its potential is limitless. When the sex emotion is redirected to the spoken word, this emotion gives feeling and the essential emotional qualities to assure effectiveness of the speech. An effective voice tone is essential. Sex emotion is the power behind all creative vision and given to humans by the Creator. Sex is the second greatest emotion that inspires. Love is first.

Your personality encompasses your mental, spiritual, and physical traits, which differentiates you from anyone else. You, and you alone, have the power to have a personality that is an asset or liability, one that attracts or repels. When making the decision to choose what type of personality you want, remember it will be the gateway in which you negotiate through life and it will largely determine your ability to cooperate with others with minimal resistance.

Let's briefly analyze a famous individual with a pleasing personality, that aided in gaining large amounts of success, Oprah Winfrey. The Oprah Winfrey Show shot up to the number one ranking, surpassing Phil Donohue in the 1980's. This was during a time when, African American women did not have their own television shows. However, everyone loved Oprah, all people. She has a positive mental attitude, charisma, the gift of effective communication, a pleasing personality.

When I reflect on my own personal experiences and interactions with people who are extremely successful, the vast majority have very attractive personalities. Those with positive mental attitudes and agreeable personalities are often found in positions of authority and responsibility or higher-income brackets. These winning personality types find very little challenge selling themselves successfully in every single relationship they encounter.

The three key traits of an attractive personality are smile, facial expression, and tone of voice. Implement these at once. Traits of a pleasing personality will contribute greatly to leading a rich, fulfilling life. These traits will improve your relationships with your children, family, friends, and colleagues. This has to be the simplest chapter to implement into your life. The cost is zero. It merely requires effort by you. This just may be the most impactful chapter in this book because it represents the nucleus of your life. Implement one pleasing personality trait at a time, until you possess them all, and watch your relationships with people and life transform.

"Power is like being a lady. . .If you have to tell people you are, you aren't."

Margaret Thatcher

CHAPTER SIX
LEVEL UP!
DRESS FOR THE LIFE YOU WANT.

"Girls of all kinds can be beautiful—from the thin, to the plus-sized, short, and very tall; the quirky, clumsy, shy, outgoing, and all in between. It's not easy though, because many people still put beauty into a confining, narrow box. Think outside of the box. Pledge that you will look in the mirror and find the unique beauty in you."

Tyra Banks

THE VAST MAJORITY of people in this world are judgmental. People will form opinions about you within the first ten seconds of meeting. This perception is typically impacted by your personal appearance, including clothing, greeting and handshake. Once we leave our home, we are under a microscope, whether we like it or not. Let me preface by saying, I am not here to judge its righteousness, but it exists. We have all encountered judgment, be it positive or negative. Societal scrutiny is not something that will soon be erased. The point is, which side of judgement do you want to be on. Will it be a hindrance or will it be a benefit to your life?

Think about it, you will be far more likely to be taken seriously if you are dressed like an adult as opposed to a teenage skateboarder or the hired help. Time to Level Up!

Dress for the life you want!

"You never get a second chance to make a first impression."
Unknown.

We've all heard the saying: dress for the job that you want and/or dress for the life you want. And you should. When you dress in the role you aspire to be in, people will begin to naturally see you there. When putting in extra effort, you are deemed as taking things seriously. It is the power of suggestion. If you are envisioned by others as in that role, the next natural step would be for you to be in that role.

Suggestion: "A psychological process in which people are manipulated by a scene, an image, a word, or a situation." Advertisers and marketers do it all the time to influence buying behavior.

The Power of Suggestion: The process by which the physical or mental state is influenced by a thought or idea. Expectations and suggestions often unconsciously change behaviors and responses, and play a major role in bringing the intended outcome into reality.

As you go out into the world daily, you are not only representing yourself; you are representing your children, family, and ancestors, which can have an impact on generations. Think bigger. Look beyond yourself.

Time to Level Up!

"Level up. Level up. Level up. Level up. Level up."
~ Ciara

This Queen coined this phrase that has become an anthem for women. Take note, ladies. Ciara is walking, breathing proof, that "Leveling Up," is real, and results are astounding.

"Them old mistakes are gone; I won't do them no more.
That's old news, there's new news. I done did that before.
I turned them into something, my comeback on one hunnid.
Less talking, more action, you just gon' CiCi coming.
I just keep elevating, no losses, just upgrading.
My lessons made blessings; I turned that into money.
Thank God I never settled; this view is so much better.
I'm chilling, I'm winning, like on another level.
You can talk all you want.
See me, I see greater.
Nothing I'm afraid of
And I can have it all. . ."
Level Up - Ciara

Positive Impact of Leveling Up.

Compliments

We all know that children are extremely honest and can be our biggest critics. So when they say something, complementary or not, you know it's true. One weekday, I was attending my daughter's away basketball game at a local school in San Francisco. I was dressed in dark blue jeans, a Chanel style jacket, with a mix of leather and wool material, paired with pointed toes flats (FYI: Jacket and pants were both from a discount store). I completed my makeup look with a pink and hint of purple lipstick, and my hair had loose curls. As I sat in the chair, waiting for the game to begin, an adorable girl with blonde hair, about eight years old, approached me and said, "You look like a Princess." I was so flattered to receive such a sweet compliment from the little girl. Feeling good absolutely comes from within; however, there is something to be said about the effort you put into your outer-self. When you look good, you feel good.

Blessings

Be open and receptive to receive. One weekday afternoon, my daughter and I visited a delicious, healthy cafe in a nice neighborhood located in San Francisco. It was the type of place where you see all of your food options and choose what you want. You are allowed to sample anything you select and I absolutely did. Following my pre-meal, I chose a kale cesar salad, buffalo cauliflower, and fried chicken. My daughter ordered chicken and broccoli. She had taken her meal and sat down to eat. When I got to the register to pay, after checking my purse, I realized I had left my wallet in the car. I told the cashier what happened and offered to go get my wallet and come right back to pay. His reply was, "No. That's okay! Don't worry about it." Again, I said, "I can go get it from my car." To which he responded again, "Don't worry about it." As you can see I was a bit insistent, at first. Then I realized, this was a blessing, and I was open to receiving. I thanked him sincerely and sat down to enjoy my meal.

Would I have gotten the same offer to not pay had I left my house looking unkempt? I don't know. But what I do know is that I did not have my meals offered to me while looking disheveled. The value was $35, and I was able to add that amount to my Money Manifestation account (See Chapter 11, The $500 Plan).

There are many more examples of blessings and compliments that I encounter regularly, and it is no coincidence. But don't take my word for it, you owe it to yourself to try it. When I leave the house feeling put together, I just feel better.

Combined with a pleasing personality is simply a winning combination. It works for me, and I know that it will be of great benefit to you.

Femininity

Qualities or attributes regarded as womanly characteristics, like prettiness, receiving, and intuition.

Femininity and women are synonymous. Femininity is an incredible blessing that comes with being a woman. With endless tasks of life, especially single motherhood, so many women have moved away from being feminine. It can be a challenge. I get it! There is no doubt that we are strong; we bring life into the world and multitask. There is nothing more powerful than that. Having strength is a given. However, femininity is a gift. It is the birthright of every woman. Reclaim it. Embrace it.

The Psychology

Enclothed cognition captures the systematic influence that clothing has on the wearer's psychological processes. Clothing can enhance (or not) our psychological status and it can improve (or not) our performance tasks.

Cognitive psychologists Hajo Adam and Adam Galinksy, from Northwestern University examined the psychological and performance-related effects that wearing specific articles of clothing have on the person wearing them. The results were quite interesting.

Adam and Galinsky gathered three groups of participants to test for heightened attention. The coats used were identical.

One group was told to wear a doctor's coat.

Another group was told to wear an artistic painter's coat.

The last group was told to look at the doctor's coat that laid across the table in front of them briefly once they entered.

Next each group was asked to perform four visual search tasks. They looked at a pair of similar pictures to spot four minor differences. Then, they were to write down each difference as quickly as possible. The participants who wore doctor's coats found more differences than those wearing the painter's coat and the subjects who were told to look at the doctor's coat. This indicated heightened attention.

In short, researchers believe that clothing holds meaning that is symbolic. The claim is that clothing influence depends both on whether or not one is wearing it, and the meaning it evoked is in one's psychological composition. When people ascribe symbolic meaning to clothing or an article thereof, and wear it, it can have an immeasurable effect. Prime example - What does the general population think about doctors? They are usually regarded as highly intelligent, scientific, and successful. The test subjects embodied the expectations of the clothing they were wearing.

There are many other studies that have shown, wearing nice clothing to work, and out in general, can affect the way people see you. Countless studies have shown when one is dressed well, confidence increases as well as the ability to think abstractly. Scientists have shown how we feel about ourselves oftentimes is linked to our personal appearance. One can literally dress for success! The clothing itself is symbolic and creates an impact on one's self-confidence and behavior.

Other considerations when selecting the clothing you wear.

1. **Wear clothing that fits the body that you have, now.**

Just because Rhianna is wearing it, does not mean that you should too. RiRi is awesome! However, her life is not our life. Rhianna has secured her financial future, and everyone knows it, so she can pretty much wear whatever she wants. Rhianna will likely always get treated well because, well, she's Rhianna.

Also note that she looked and dressed very differently when she was a new artist. Once Rhianna secured her future, she dressed and did whatever she wanted.

It is important to wear clothing that fits properly and flatters your body type. Find a good tailor (cleaners will often provide this service). Clothing customized to fit your body perfectly amplifies your overall look. I'm not talking about custom couture. This service can actually be quite affordable. I pay about $14 for a pant hem. I also have dresses and blazers tailored to fit. For me less is more. I'd much rather have four pairs of pants that fit flawlessly, that I love wearing, versus twenty that are ill-fitting, that I dread to even look at.

2. Dress for the season.

Dress appropriately for the weather. In doing so, you will always remain comfortable, sensible, and stylish. Choose quality over quantity.

3. Dress for the occasion.

I want you to say aloud, "Leggings are for the gym!" One more time. . . Great! Glad that is out of the way. Forgo the temptation to wear those ultra-comfy, made for exercise, leggings. I'm not going to even discuss pajamas outside of your home. Just, don't. You wouldn't wear a tennis skirt to play basketball in. If you are attending a business meeting, networking event or an interview, wear business attire that makes you feel confident and intelligent. This will likely be professional wear i.e. a suit. Attending a social gathering at the park with the kiddos, opt for jeans for a more casual look. Find your style icon – use Pinterest, Instagram or the World Wide Web for inspiration.

Appearance and clothing tell a personal story about you. What story do you want to tell people?

As you get dressed and are tending to your personal grooming, consider what you will be communicating to people. Examine everything, from nails (color/length), hair (color/length/style), what you smell like and of course, clothing. Ask yourself, "Am I sending the message that I am attempting to project?" If not, take inventory of yourself and make modifications.

Just how much do looks matter? We are judged not only by how we look, but also how we dress, table manners, weight and grooming.

Surprising Stats

More evidence that putting effort into your personal appearance is worth the extra effort.

1. People deemed fat, get paid less:

Obese employees, on average, are paid less than their "normal-weight" counterparts at a rate of $8,666 per year for obese women, according to a study at George Washington University. Other studies have indicated, women who are obese are even more likely to be discriminated against as it relates to hiring, raises, and pay.

Tyra Banks conducted her own experiment in 2005 on her talk show. She was transformed into a 350-pound obese woman. Tyra expressed in an AP Radio interview, "It was one of the most heartbreaking days of my life. The people that were staring and laughing in my face – that shocked me the most. As soon as I entered the store—when I went shopping—I immediately heard snickers. Immediately!" Tyra also went on several blind dates to which she says one was outright rude and hurtful. She asked the second date what his parents would say if he brought her home to meet them. He responded, "They'll be like, What's wrong with you?" Once Tyra revealed her identity to the third prospect, he admitted he would not have gone out with her again as a 350-pound woman.

Size is not merely about superficialities; there is also health to consider. You want to be mobile and at the healthiest version of self not just for you but for your children.

2. People who work out get paid more:

The Journal of Labor Research reports that workers who exercise on a regular basis earn on average, nine percent more than employees that do not work out. A similar study from Cleveland State University claims people that exercise three or more times a week earn an average of $80 more a week than their inactive colleagues. It's almost as if you are getting paid to exercise. Cha-ching! One could argue that endorphins released when we exercise contribute to a more pleasing personality, better attitude, and more energy which could equate to higher pay. Either way, working out is beneficial!

3. Women that wear makeup, make more money:

Women who wear make-up also rank higher in competence and trustworthiness, according to a study funded by Harvard Medical School, Procter & Gamble, Massachusetts General Hospital, Boston University, and the Dana-Farber Cancer Institute. According to a study in the American Economic Review, women who wear makeup can earn more than thirty percent more in pay than non-makeup wearing workers.

Women are judged by their looks. No shocker there. What is surprising is that the number of cosmetic surgical procedures have continued to skyrocket in the United States over the past five years. According to the American Society of Plastic Surgeons (ASPS), nearly 18 million people underwent surgical and minimally invasive cosmetic procedures in the United States in 2018.

Obviously, undergoing cosmetic enhancement is totally a personal choice, and number three is completely about makeup. But, I would be remiss if I failed to mention this data is an example of how obsessed about looks as a society we have truly become. Keep in mind, there is also statistical data citing many people who undergo these procedures suffer from self-esteem challenges. This is why it is extremely important to always be working on the inner-self as well, (See chapter 5, Pleasing Personality). Confidence of self, combined with a pleasing personality, beats out a visually, perfectly-constructed individual, any day. Exercise, healthy food intake (eating to live), lots of water, proper skincare regime with a sprinkle of makeup can do wonders ladies, without medical enhancements.

4. Beautiful people are paid beautifully:

According to a study at Yale University by Daniel Hamermesh, he finds employers pay a physical attractiveness premium to employees. Unattractive employees can miss out on up to nine percent, while beautiful workers earn approximately five percent more.

I don't believe in unattractive women, just lazy, unaware, or perhaps time impoverished. Why would I say this? If a masculine man can apply makeup to his face and look drop-dead gorgeous, we can do it too. Don't believe me, take a trip to YouTube. Many of the men apply their makeup way better than I ever could and the end results are fabulous.

We have all judged someone at some point in our lives, strictly based on looks, be it positively or negatively. If you dress "nicely" so infrequently, that people you know compliment you and ask where you are going. You may be underdressing. Again, how do you want to be perceived?

Not only do I want to represent myself in a certain way for me; I want to be an example for my child and family. My daughter asked me for a month straight where I was going, or did I have a meeting when I dropped her off at school in the morning. I explained to her, this was the new me and that it takes the same amount of time to put on a dress or nice jumpsuit as it does to put on leggings and they are both similarly comfortable. I'm happy to report; I no longer get asked that question.

Kids absorb everything. As they grow, whether we like it or not, they will begin to mimic us either in a subtle or drastic manner. The goal is for children to mirror positive habits and traits. This will include how you groom yourself, the clothing you put on your body, how you take care of yourself, and the confidence you exude as a result.

It's all in appearances.

Have you ever observed a man dressed very basic; jeans, t-shirt, partially groomed hair, and beard? Then, Abracadabra! Next you see the same man dressed in a suit with a clean-shaven haircut and beard while smelling good. Big difference. With the change, you may find yourself staring at him, wanting to talk to him, and inhaling his fragrant scent. Humans are visual creatures and the effort we put into ourselves can make a big difference. Revisit your five senses while getting dressed: visual, scent, taste, touch (skin and hair care), and voice. We can't all wake up flawless like Beyonce, Naomi Campbell or Blake Lively. Some of us actually have to put in some effort. And what a difference a little effort makes!

The "Level Up" is transformational. There is something to be said about, when you look good, you feel good. Everything will begin to change. You will have a glow about you that people will notice and gravitate toward. Confidence will soar. You will begin to walk and talk differently. It's all quite magical.

"The level up is about improving, not impressing. Show yourself that you can get better. It's you versus you at the end of the day."

Unknown.

CHAPTER SEVEN
HOW TO ASK FOR WHAT YOU WANT - AND GET IT!

"Am I bossy? Absolutely. I don't like to lose, and if I'm told "no", then I find another way to get my 'yes."

Naomi Campbell

ASK!

I promise you that most successful women know how to ask for what they want.

Ask and you shall receive. Imagine the person you are asking is a genie and you expect them to grant your wish. Ask with clarity and confidence. Claim your wish with gratitude.

What's the worst that can happen when you ask for something? You will hear the word 'no.' I'm sure your kids have told you 'no' many, many times. Nothing new there. Ask, and get what you want!

Have you ever heard the saying, "A closed mouth doesn't get fed?" There are proven statistics that show women ask for what they want less than men. One study tested the gender difference by telling the participants they would be paid $3 - $10 dollars for playing a game, while being observed. After each person completed the game they were told, "Here's $3. Is $3 okay?" The majority of women passively accepted the $3.

In fact, one woman for every nine men requested more money. Women are conditioned at a young age to focus on others' needs ahead of their own. We often think that we will receive what we deserve, without asking, which most often is not the case. Let's control our outcome. Here's how.

1. Ask with the expectation that you will receive.

Begin with a confident level of certainty and high expectations when you are asking for what you want. Ask with the mindset that you have already received it. Thoughts become things. Your mental state is the foundation, and it will affect your outward actions; body posture, eye contact, tone of voice and choice of words. Confidence is key. Channel a time when you've asked for something with confidence and got it!

2. Make a reasonable request (sort of).

It's a challenge for me to say be reasonable when I believe in being limitless and shooting for the stars. However, in this case, you must have some level of reasonability. For example, you wouldn't ask a friend to borrow $20,000 if they only make $30,000 a year. Just as you would not ask for a job promotion from a nurse to a Doctor if you didn't have a doctorate degree. My examples are extreme to prove a point, be within reason. One tactic to get to yes, is to ask for more then you want/more than you think you'll receive. Begin by asking for a large favor or large sum of money that you know they will likely say no to. If and when they say no, follow up with a much smaller request which is what you were hoping to receive. In order to not seem uncaring or cheap, it is likely they will agree to the smaller ask. A smaller amount or smaller ask will seem minuscule in comparison. You may even get your inflated, initial ask. This has happened to me before.

Choose this strategy if it is right for your situation and the individual. This tactic can be an effective marketing strategy, but it can have the opposite effect, particularly in personal relationships. Determine if your ask is within the individuals, capacity and if it's something they will do for you.

3. Baby, I'm worth it!

Start by telling yourself that you're worth it. Studies have shown that women who are hesitant to ask for pay raises feel that deep inside, they don't deserve a higher salary. Think about and determine why you are afraid to make the request you are contemplating. Do you feel inadequate? Have you been conditioned to feel you don't deserve it? Examine why you are fearful of the ask. Feel the fear and do it anyway. Prepare first (See number 4).

4. Write down your request.

Have a list of reasons why you should get a, 'Yes!' Create win-win scenarios whenever possible. Organize your thoughts in writing.

5. Be sure you are asking the person who can give what you are asking for.

It is imperative you ask the 'right' person. So, prior to asking, assess whether or not they have the ability or authority to give you what you are asking. What capacity does she or he have? You want the decision-maker, someone with the authority to give you what you want. There will be times when you will need to bypass people, as their capacity may be limited.

6. Wait until they are in a happy place (mentally).

When we want our requests fulfilled, the focus can tend to be more, 'I-centered.' Observe non-verbal cues. Do they appear troubled or preoccupied? Are you adding another pile to their plate? A person is more likely to say yes when they are feeling great. Imagine being at your most favorite place in the world or eating your favorite dish. How do you feel when you are in those moments? Divine! That is exactly the place where you want to catch the "askie", in their happy place.

Think about when your child asks for something while you are in a good mood. Does your response and reaction differ when you are in a bad mood? Likely, so consider mood when you are asking for something.

7. Have full attention.

Do not be multi-tasked! When a person is bogged down with multiple things it makes it easier for them to dismiss your ask. Request to wait or schedule an appointment for a time in the near future when they can give you their full consideration.

8. Be concise and to the point.

Clarity is essential during the ask. Ask for what you want, and DO NOT include what you don't want. The only thing that matters is what you want. Write out exactly what it is you want. Practice in the mirror until you are comfortable and confident. You've got this! Have you ever heard the saying, "Be careful of what you ask for? You just might get it." Be precise and succinct, to ensure you get exactly what you want.

9. The request should come from your heart.

You can have anything you want, if you want it bad enough. It is essential to have desire, followed by unwavering faith that you are going to get it. When you speak of that which you want, exude trustworthiness and let your passion shine through. Be creative. Charm, disarms defenses and opens the mind to new possibilities. Always be charming.

10. Give something to get something.

Where ever possible, you want to create win-win situations. Empathize with the person's point of view and emotions. While asking, explain how this will be beneficial, enhance, or how she or he will win because they acted positively on your request. For example, when you are interviewing for a new job, you not only want to express how wonderful an opportunity it would be to be hired, but how your employment will enhance the company.

11. How to ask vulnerably and directly?

If it wasn't business or directly related to my daughter or brother, I was the queen of the indirect ask. Asking for things for yourself, puts you in a very vulnerable position, even when it's something you need. Whether you are sick, need assistance with pick up, or just need a break from doing everything yourself. Single moms often have the mindset that these things are not essential and so we manage them ourselves. Asking for help leaves you open to rejection. As single moms, we tend to avoid vulnerability. Let's break the cycle together.

So, what is the most effective way to ask?

Would you be willing to. . .

(magical)

'Would you be willing to', is so much more inviting. This language relaxes defenses. Demanding language often makes people defensive, 'Can you do XYZ for me,' which we try to avoid. State your vulnerability, what you need help with, followed by the ask.

Examples:

I am feeling very stressed because I need support with drop-offs and pick-ups. Would you be willing to pick Jordan up from school on Fridays?

I haven't heard back from you, which makes me feel anxious. Would you be willing to reassure me you received my messages, and respond as soon as you are able to?

Requests should specify, measure and be time-sensitive so that the person who received the request has a chance to meet the request successfully. The more specific the better; it avoids misunderstanding the request.

Give options whenever possible.

Humans like choices; they allow us to feel as if we have some form of control. Especially when you are asking the humans with big egos. Ahem...I wonder which human species that is? Would you be willing to put together Sarah's bike and doll house by Sunday (Four days later) or pay for the store to do it?

Would you be willing to pay for Sarah's ballet classes or taekwondo lessons?

12. The person who asks the questions, is the one that controls the conversation.

Asking questions is an excellent way to control communication. When you ask questions, you are commanding an answer, though it is not obvious to the one being asked. Steer the conversation in the direction you choose with a barrage of questions. This is an effective negotiating technique. It leaves less room for the individual to think of a rebuttal. Ask open ended questions that require more than a mere, yes or no answer. This forces the individual to think, recollect and respond.

My lease renewal was up on my apartment and I wanted my living room repainted upon signing the new lease. So, I decided to approach the manager in person for the request. First. I provided the foundation. As a long-standing tenant, that pays rent on time I asked to have my living room repainted. "No, we can't do that." was the manager's response. Can't! Well in my mind, I know there was no such thing as, can't. Besides, my bathroom was repainted one-year prior upon lease renewal, so no just would not do. I began by asking for the reason why she was declining my request. She gave me an answer that I do not recall. So, I asked another question, and another, and another. By the end of my questions, she responded with, "We can paint the living room, but only with the white color we use." She thought I would be saddened by the idea of not being able to use my own paint choice as I purchased another paint color for the bathroom, the year prior. Little did she know, I was more than happy to use their free, white paint for my living room. I looked slightly disappointed to make her think she had won, and with a slight hesitation I said, "Okay, I guess white will have to do. Thank you." When in doubt, ask more questions.

Lesson 1

A lesson in persistence and tenacity. Robert Smith, an American investor and businessman got the yes. While in high school, Smith applied for an internship at Bell Labs, which was intended for a college student. Smith confidently declared that he would do a better job than any college student could. He was told, no. Smith called to speak with the hiring manager every day for several weeks, followed by once a week, for six months. Every phone call, the secretary responded with, "May I take a message, please." So, each and every phone call Smith politely left his name and number. The day came that Smith got his chance when a M.I.T. student did not show up for the internship. Smith, finally succeeded in obtaining the internship, despite six months of no's. In 2018, Smith was ranked by Forbes as the 163rd richest person in America.

Lesson 2

Think of the persistent child. "Mommy! Mommy! Can I have another juice box, please?" This, after they have already had four in the past hour. "No." "Mommy! Mommy! *Pleeeze.* . .Just one more, I promise I won't ask again. I Love you so much, Mommy. You are the *bestest* Mommy ever." Then we cave. Whether it's a story like Robert Smith's or a story like this one, kids don't give up easily when they want something. Be persistent like the child.

By passively asking for what we want, we are often misinterpreted and our wants remain unmet. If our request goes unheard and unanswered, we have only ourselves to blame. It is not the fault of our boss, business associates, ex, family or friends if we did not ask specifically and directly. No two minds are alike and you cannot expect someone to read yours. Merely presenting a problem or a situation to someone will not always warrant them to jump in to help if nothing is asked of them.

Make your efforts worth it. If you take the time to put yourself out there, just ask. You deserve it and you are worth it. You can have your needs and wants met by your boss, colleagues and loved ones. Remember, you have nothing to lose and everything to gain. What is the risk versus the reward? In most cases, the risk is a simple, no. We've all heard the word "no" before, and it's all good. But the reward can be limitless: a raise, more time off from work, more time with your family, more time for yourself, more help with your child's expenses. The sky's the limit!!

Take it from a recovering Super Mom. I'm here to tell you vulnerability is a beautiful thing. When people see that you are human and not infallible, they want to help. So, get out there and ask for what you want. Moms, you are beyond deserving.

Bonus Tip!

The more persuasive you are, the better. Sometimes, you will have to include a few sprinkles of finesse. The more tips from this chapter you include, the higher the likelihood of 'Yes!' Keep in mind, you will encounter 'no', just like Mr. Smith. You may even have to approach the same individual repeatedly before you get to 'yes.' With tenacity and persistence, you also can get to, 'Yes!'

"Ask for what you want, and be prepared to get it."
Maya Angelou

CHAPTER EIGHT
ADULTING 101
FINANCIAL PLANNING AND PREPARING
FOR A BETTER TOMORROW.

"For tomorrow belongs to people who prepare for it today."
African Proverb

So, FEW PEOPLE actually "get rich quick." Wealth building is a marathon, not a sprint. This chapter focuses on planning for life, preparing for death and everything in between.

Life Insurance

Life insurance is for the living, not the dead. Ensure your children will be financially taken care of should anything happen. At a bare minimum every mom should have life insurance coverage for herself. Consider having a policy for each child. In many cases, once children reach a certain age (typically 18-21) a cash value becomes available which could be used for college, investing or a business your child wants to start. Because children are young and healthy, the cost will start at approximately $5 for the smallest policy. The sooner you purchase life insurance the better. As we age the cost of premiums increase. Let's face it, the younger you are, the healthier you are. In essence, the insurance company's money is safer.

Whole Life Insurance versus Term Life Insurance

Whole life insurance covers the individual until death and accumulates a cash value. The monthly cost of this policy is more expensive than term insurance because coverage is until death. The cost is approximately double that of term insurance.

Term life insurance covers the individual for a certain period of time usually 20-30 years. The cost for this type of insurance policy is often very affordable. This option works great if you do not have a huge budget right now, this choice will enable you to have a policy that will cover you at a reasonable cost. You can always choose to add additional policies later. Average cost: $15-$100 per month for policies ranging $20,000-$800,000.

Automobile Insurance

Auto insurance is mandatory if you live in the United States. Many states have required legal minimums. Beyond those minimums, coverage amounts are determined by you.

Liability insurance covers the cost of damage you cause to others while driving. For example, you would be responsible for medical costs for individuals injured in the accident and/or repair costs of damage to other vehicles if you were determined at fault. Liability insurance does not cover your vehicle in most cases.

Full coverage will also cover the cost of your vehicle and what is listed above under liability insurance. This coverage is comprehensive and collision insurance.

Comprehensive coverage assists in paying to replace or repair your vehicle if it were stolen or damaged by a natural disaster, falling objects, vandalism, fire, flood, etc. Essentially, it covers damage to the automobile outside of driving.

Collision insurance is damage caused while driving like hitting a car or object.

Policies vary greatly depending upon the type of car you own and your age. Tip: If you are in the market for buying a car, call the insurance company to get quotes on the types of cars you are interested in. The insurance quote may steer your purchasing decision.

Pro Tip: Self-made multi-millionaires, Kevin O'Leary, Suze Orman and Dr. George Fraser say you should never buy a brand-new car. The car drops in value by thirty percent the moment you drive it off of the lot. Most people borrow money to buy this depreciating asset. But seriously, who has thirty percent to just give away? Consider buying a low mileage newer car. Dr Fraser and his wife made an agreement to never buy a brand-new car. They instead took the additional monies they would have paid monthly for a new car payment and invested it for forty-eight years straight. Brilliant.

Renters Insurance

Renters insurance protects your personal property, personal liability, and damage or bodily injuries to others. It also covers lodging (hotel) and meal allowances should you need to vacate your home. I had to use renter's insurance once and my only wish is that I had a higher policy because I was out of my home for thirty days and renters insurance coverage was $3500, which wasn't enough. On the upside, it was summer and I was able to rent a hotel room in Hawaii as opposed to my own city. Vacation time!! When I asked my agent if I could use my rental allowance to stay in Hawaii, the response was, "Hmm... I've never been asked that question before. But, what a great idea! I will check with my manager and get back to you." Approved!! Renters insurance is rather inexpensive and so worth the money. The cost is on average $100-$300 per year. Note: the landlord may be responsible for covering your lodging; however, they may want to put you in lodging that is below your standard of living, so having choices is comforting.

Homeowners Insurance

Basic homeowner's insurance covers damage to property, belongings and personal liability. The policy pays to repair or rebuild the home if it is damaged or destroyed by disasters listed in the policy. Most standard policies cover financial loss caused by weather and catastrophic events and accidents. Everything listed in renter's insurance above is typically covered in homeowners insurance. Note: if your state is prone to specific natural disasters, you will likely have to pay an additional premium for your policy to cover it.

Short-term disability insurance

Short-term disability insurance replaces a portion of your paycheck for a short period of time. Think three to six months. Most people get STDI through their employer. You can get an individual policy through some private insurers, but these plans generally cost more than they're worth.

A solution to STDI would be to have a separate savings account for unplanned life events to offset having this type of insurance.

Long-term Disability Insurance

This policy protects an employee from income loss if they become unable to work for a long time period because of an illness, accident or injury. Should one become disabled, a percentage of their income would be paid. The percentage of income received depends upon the policy chosen. Disability insurance can often be purchased through your employment. Private insurance is also an option. Cost is typically, one to three percent of your income. Dave Ramsey (New York Times best-selling author of Total Money Makeover) recommends long term disability insurance as a must.

Tip: Most insurance companies offer multiple policy discounts.

Health Care insurance is very important. Costs for out of pocket expenses can be astronomical in the United States.

Where to get Health Coverage:

1. Check with your employer first.
2. Ask your child's father to add your child to their coverage (get dual coverage if you can).
3. Visit your county's Human Services Agency. If your income is low, you and your children may be entitled to free or low-cost health insurance.
4. Private insurance (You would pay out of pocket).

Flexible Spending Account (FSA) = Tax Free Health

Most people are not fully covered under medical and dental insurance. Health Care FSA is a pre-tax benefit account that is used to pay for eligible medical, dental and vision care expenses that are not covered by your insurance plan. With Health Care Flexible Spending Account (HCFSA), you use pre-tax dollars to pay for qualified out-of-pocket health care expenses. This account is available to government employees and offered by some employers. Ask your employer or visit www.fsafeds.com to learn more about the Flexible Spending Account.

Custodial Account

A custodial account is a savings account opened on behalf of a minor and controlled by an adult. The child is the legal owner of this account from the beginning, even though an adult opens it. The advantage of a custodial account is that the funds can be used not only for education but for buying real estate, starting a business or continued investment and growth. When the child becomes an adult, they get full control of the account. Although, you may be able to designate when they can access the funds up to twenty-five years of age. This account can be opened at a financial institution, mutual fund company or brokerage firm. Gift the account weekly or monthly amounts, ongoing. When people ask what your child wants for their birthday or during holidays, you could ask them to gift the custodial account.

Plant the seeds early. Talk to your child about the importance of saving and encourage them to save fifty percent of all money they receive or earn. Whether your child begins earning money inside of the home (via allowance), through employment or entrepreneurship, they can also contribute to their own account and watch it grow. Observing the amazing growth over time is a great incentive to continue saving.

401(k)

This account is for people who plan to be impoverished when they retire. However, if employers offer to match your contributions, it makes sense to take advantage of that free money.

Typically, it is assumed that income will go down once you retire, in which case you will be taxed at a lower tax bracket. However, if you are wealthy when you retire, you could pay higher taxes on your 401(k).

The 401(k) company makes money even when you do not. As the investor you put up all of the money and take all of the risk. According to TIME Magazine, plan administrators are taking one cent from every dollar that Americans hold in their 401(k) annually. Compounded over an entire career and that is a whole lot of money the investors lose out on. TIME also noted many other concerns with this outdated retirement savings plan.

Most financial advisors of these pension plans are merely employees doing a job, not skilled investors. However, they are paid to manage massive amounts of money, in which they have no vested interest in. I don't know about you, but I'm betting on myself over a stranger. In subsequent chapters to find out how you can make your money work for you.

Roth IRA

A Roth IRA is an individual retirement account which you contribute after tax money. This account offers tax-free growth and tax-free withdrawals in retirement. You pay taxes on the money before it goes into the account. Once you retire you can withdraw those funds tax free.

Many banking institutions offer Roth IRA's. Keep in mind this option has annual income limits, approximately $124,000 for a single person. Select a company such as Vanguard or Charles Schwab and choose stock investments for your retirement portfolio.

Will & Trust

A will is a document that takes effect once you die. It gives direction as to who will receive what property once deceased. In addition to property, a designation of whom would become guardian of the children would be included. Lastly, choose an executor to carry out the terms of the will. Conversely, a trust is effective the moment you create it. It is a legal arrangement in which a "trustee" is designated to hold legal titles to property for beneficiaries (such as a bank or a law firm). A trust can begin to make distributions before death, or after.

Why is having a will so important? If there is no will in place, the family will likely have to hire an attorney and go to probate court to claim assets. Should this happen, attorney's will be entitled to three to seven percent of the estate, and it could take several years to settle. This process can take a toll on the decedents, especially if they disagree. It can literally tear a family apart. I've seen it first-hand. I implore you to draft a will for your children. They deserve to grieve with peace of mind.

How to make an informed choice when choosing an insurance company.

There are four main rating agencies to aid you in selecting the best policy for your needs. They are:

- A.M. Best Company: www.ambest.com
- Standard & Poor's: www.standardandpoors.com
- Moody's: www.moodys.com
- Fitch: www.fitchratings.com

These rating agencies consider a company's financials, recent performance, management stability and overall financial health, as well as external factors such as competition, market presence and diversification. Not all insurance companies are rated by all four. However, if a company is rated favorably by at least three it will likely be a solid choice. Financial strength ratings are useful; however, they are not a guarantee of an insurer's financial strength and stability. Do your own due diligence and research, and use common sense when selecting an insurance company. I personally go with larger, more reputable companies that have been around for many, many years.

You want to be sure to get insurance that you can afford, now. You want plans with amounts that will be paid consistently and on time. The goal is not to be "insurance rich" and "cash poor." Find a happy balance. Spend time reading and researching before you decide on a plan. Insurance can be paid monthly, quarterly, or annually.

Many employers offer Disability insurance, Health Care insurance and Life insurance. Check with them first. Life insurance through your employer can often be minimal coverage. However, take advantage of all that your employer has to offer. If you need more coverage than what your employer offers, you can always get more from outside sources.

Start now. You can always make changes and adjustments later.

The best benefit is peace of mind. Having a prepared plan that contains instructions that will protect your family and your assets is very important. Having insurance, investments, and savings, along with a plan, is one of the most thoughtful, loving and adult acts you can do for yourself and children.

"Plan for what is difficult while it is easy, do what is great while it is small."

Szu Tzu

CHAPTER NINE
Budgeting
The road to financial independence.

"A budget is more than just a series of numbers on a page; it is an embodiment of our values."

Barack Obama

IT IS IMPORTANT to know where you are financially, in order to have a clear picture of where you need to go to achieve your goals. Having a budget is the difference between controlling your finances or allowing your finances to control you. Either you tell your money what to do or it will tell you what you cannot do.

Financial Independence begins with budgeting.

Financial Independence is having enough income to pay for all living expenses without having a job or being dependent on anyone else, by way of passive income and investments. One can choose to be employed; however, it is by choice as opposed to necessity. For example, Beyonce continues to work (performing at concerts, creating product lines, etc.) but it is not essential for her survival. Beyonce has reached financial independence. The beauty is, Beyonce can choose work that she loves, to continue to increase her wealth. Having choices is the ideal place to be.

Being financially independent simply gives you more options. You can choose to spend more time with your loved ones, travel or quit a job you despise. It all begins with budgeting.

Stop Spending. Can you really afford that?

Ask yourself: Can I purchase XYZ without first checking my bank account? Can I pay all of my bills with ease, and without flinching? Do I have zero credit card or student loan debt? Most importantly, do you have a budget? If you answered no to any one of those questions, and do not currently have a budget and your goal is to become financially free, stop spending.

But, why? Chances are, you are sabotaging your financial freedom if you are not aware of where your money is going and you have no assets to show for it. Just to be clear, a car is not an asset. I would never say, "You have debt, never spend again." I'm a huge believer in buying items that bring joy that are valued and appreciated. As a recovering shopaholic it took some time to get here. I came to the realization that less is more. Shopping is not a hobby, unless you are Rockefeller. It didn't make good sense for me to own 100 pairs of shoes, when I only really wore ten pairs regularly. It was not serving my bank account or my family to spend money on expensive sneakers or outfits for a kindergartener who grows out of shoes every three to six months and ruins clothes like nobody's business. I made the conscious choice to choose quality over quantity. Experiences over things. Because, at the end of the day, when kids become adults, they will remember the quality of the time spent with you versus the designer brands they wore. The money that you would have spent on expensive clothing/toys could go into a custodial account for your child, for investing or for college. Now, that's a return on your investment!

Budgeting Basics

The hardest part about creating a budget is starting. A good budget can help monitor spending, discover hidden expenses and define financial goals like investing or saving for a home.

Know where your money is going *every* month down to the penny! This may sound daunting, but it is important to document it all. This includes fixed monthly bills like rent/mortgage, insurance, student loans, cell phone, credit cards, gas and electricity and bills that fluctuate like, groceries, fast food/dining out, clothing, entertainment/recreation, children's activities, etc. I like to include interest percentages next to my credit cards and student loans, so that I know how much additional monies I'm paying. Write it all down by hand or digitally. Next, include all income from employment, child support, freelance jobs, etc. Include all savings, investments and retirement accounts.

Use this budget template as a guide to your financial freedom:

BUDGET TEMPLATE:

MONTHLY BUDGET					
Income		Budgeted	Due Date		Actual
Beginning Balance	$	500.00		$	500.00
Active Income					
Income 1	$	2,200.00		$	2,200.00
Income 2	$	500.00		$	600.00
Income 3	$	250.00		$	350.00
Income 4					
Income 5					
Passive Income					
Income 1	$	225.00		$	225.00
Income 2	$	375.00		$	375.00
Income 3					
Income 4					
Income 5					
Total Income	$	4,050.00		$	4,250.00
Loans					
Car Loan	$	100.00		$	75.00
Student Loan 1					
Student Loan 2					
Loan 4					
Loan 5					
Expenses					
Rent/Mortgage	$	1,800.00		$	1,800.00
Utilities					
Internet/Cable	$	35.00		$	35.00
Car Insurance					
Life Insurance	$	20.00		$	20.00
Health Insurance	$	125.00		$	125.00
Home Insurance					
Child Care/Tuition					
Child Activity					
Food	$	350.00		$	325.00
Cell Phone					
Gas					
Bridge Toll					
Gym					
Clothes					
Salon					
Recreation					
Subscription 1					
Subscription 2					
Subscription 3					
Subscription 4					
Credit Card 1					
Credit Card 2					
Credit Card 3					
Credit Card 4					
Miscellaneous					
Savings					
Retirement	$	300.00		$	300.00
Life/Emergency Acct	$	225.00		$	225.00
Financial Goal	$	150.00		$	150.00
Lifestyle Goal	$	50.00		$	50.00
Stock Shares	$	100.00		$	100.00
Investment	$	300.00		$	1,000.00
Custodial Account	$	50.00		$	50.00
College Fund					
Total Expense	$	3,605.00		$	4,255.00
Net	$	445.00		$	(5.00)

For a free pdf of this budget template visit singlemomandthecity.com

Want the excel spreadsheet, version? Visit my Etsy store at etsy.com beautifulyousf.

Now that you have all of the figures, it's time to tell your money what you want it to do!

1. **Cancel automatic subscriptions/memberships that you do not use regularly.**

   For services that you do use, share the cost with family or friends.

2. **Reduce groceries.**

   Save money on groceries by meal planning. I find the just-in-time method useful to reduce spoilage, stockpiling and waste. I keep a small notepad in the kitchen, and when I notice that I'm running low or am out of staple food items it gets added to the list. Use grocery delivery or pickup to avoid overspending.

3. **Automate your savings and use a remote account.**

   I have found that out of sight out of mind is the most effective way of saving. Depending on the saving account, have the money deducted directly from your check monthly or from your bank account when you get paid. What's nice is that you don't really think about it, since you don't need to physically do anything monthly. In a remote account, funds are usually not readily accessible to you. It would take more effort to access the funds, versus being able to walk into your local bank for a withdrawal.

4. Bonus, tax return, or windfall.

If you know that you will be receiving a chunk of money, like an annual tax return, it's important for you to assign where you want that money to go. Pay yourself first by assigning a percentage or dollar amount to go toward your financial goals or investments. Next, start with your high-interest debt. If you are debt-free you can put more towards your financial goals and/or investments. This blessing of financial abundance has entered your life and it is only right that you are allowed a little splurge even if you have debt. Whether you choose an experience like a family day at the park with yummy food and kite flying, a facial for yourself, having the house professionally cleaned, or a new dress, choose an amount that's in line with your financial goals and future.

5. Bring your lunch.

Avoiding the additional cost of buying lunch and lattes daily could greatly decrease this expense.

6. Make your own fancy "lattes."

My drink of choice is the delicious chai tea latte. But at five to seven dollars a day, this was not a sound financial choice. So, I purchased a cute portable travel mug, milk frother and the ingredients required to recreate this delectable treat. That's a savings of over $100 per month!

7. Always ask about coupons and discounts.

Nearly every time I make a purchase, I ask about promotions or discounts. Many stores, like Target, even offer price matching. Any amounts I save, I add to, *The $500 Plan*. Find out more about, *The $500 Plan* in chapter eleven.

8. Contact your cell phone provider and ask how you can lower your bill.

See which extras you can cut. I used to get the insurance, but no more! I felt like, "Let me get this straight. I have to pay you $12 a month for insurance. Then if my phone breaks, I have to pay an additional $175 deductible to fix my phone. In addition, after just one year, I've paid you $144 for insurance for the grand total of $319. No, thanks!" I have had to get my phone serviced after two-plus years of having it. I paid a mere $75 for a battery replacement versus the $460 or more that it would have cost me if I had the insurance.

9. Sell it all!

If you have items in your life that are no longer serving you, that you don't love, sell them and make some much needed space, and money to put toward your financial goals. With items that have little to no value (or may be difficult to sell), donate.

"There is no magic to achievement. It's really about hard work, choices and persistence."

Michelle Obama

The Importance of Saving!

Always pay yourself first. You deserve it! Saving ten to fifteen percent of your income is a guideline that many experts use as a measurement of what you should save monthly. Here are great starting points for savings goals: emergency/life account (six months of living expenses), retirement, investment and custodial account. Whatever you decide to save your money for, the most important thing is to leave the money there. The point of saving is to let your money accumulate for its intended purpose. It's a good idea to automate your savings transfers to ensure the money will be saved regularly and you don't have to be actively involved in the process. If the savings account is remote, it is out of sight out of mind. You don't even miss the money because if it wasn't being saved, somehow it still gets spent. It is essential to your progress to choose a percentage or set an amount that is saved and untouched until you reach your goal. If you are new to saving, starting small may feel more doable. You can always increase the amount and add more money to your account at any time.

Single Moms make it work, no matter what! With a budget, we are going to earn, spend, and save with ease. I know it can be quite daunting to think about our income, and all the monthly expenses that have to be paid. But I promise you will feel a sense of a relief and accomplishment just to have all of the figures right in front of you, making it easier to plan for the future you want.

Without a budget, cash just kind of coasts in and out of our lives. If your money makes a grand entrance and exit each month, with nothing of significance to show a budget can help change that. The question becomes, do we want our finances to coast or soar through life? I want to see our income soar – for every single person reading this book. Abundance and financial independence, is yours!!

"Don't tell me what you value, show me your budget, and I'll tell you what you value."

Joe Biden

CHAPTER TEN
THE POWER OF
PASSIVE INCOME
CREATING INTERGENERATIONAL WEALTH.

"If you don't find a way to make money while you sleep, you will work until you die."

Warren Buffett

DO YOU WANT to be the horse or the jockey in this race called life?

Invest more in yourself than you do others.

The number one reason single moms should create passive income is time. More time to spend with children, more time for yourself, while simultaneously teaching your child how to think outside of the box when it comes to making money. Passive income is a key wealth-building tool.

Intergenerational Wealth is when an extremely large sum of money and/or assets is acquired by beneficiaries (i.e.: children) in the form of a gift or inheritance.

The average millionaire has seven streams of income. Simply put, this means they are receiving checks from seven sources, which often comes in the form of passive income.

Passive income is making money while you sleep. It is earned in a way that requires little to no daily effort to maintain. You will however have to put in upfront effort. For example, if you choose to create an online program, there would be work involved in creating the program and setting up online systems. Once the upfront investment of time is put forth, maintenance will be relatively simple. You earn your freedom with passive income.

Active income is trading time for dollars. This is the majority of the population's way of earning money. It's no wonder why a large amount of resources, belong to a small portion of people. In September 2017 a study by the Federal Reserve reported that the top one percent owned over thirty-eight percent of the country's wealth. Wow!

Passive income is ultimately the way to go. Think, Oprah Winfrey. Do you think Oprah reached billionaire status by trading her time for money? Probably not.

If you're in debt, don't fret! You're not alone, most of America is, approximately seventy-five percent. Let's talk about how to get out.

Consider the stock market. People with large amounts of money are investing in the stock market. What's amazing is that you actually don't need large amounts of money to invest. History shows that the stock market increases over time. The stock market has increased like a rocket in the last thirty to forty years.

In 1942, at age eleven, Warren Buffet made his very first investment of $114.75. He purchased three shares of Cities Service, which is no longer in existence. Buffet calculated, "If I had invested that $114.75 into a no fee, S&P 500 index fund, while reinvesting 100% of the dividends, by January 2019, my investment would be worth $606,811." Do I have your attention now?

"Little things turn into big things."

John W. Rogers Jr.

Think you need to be a stock market guru in order to invest. Nope. A monkey can do it even more successfully than a wall street stock broker, and so can you. No, really!!

In 2012, a study was conducted to show that monkeys could pick stocks simply by throwing darts and do just as well as the professionals on Wall Street. Well, the test was wrong. The monkeys did better! If the monkeys can do it, so can we. The key is to remember, you are running a long game, not a short one. So, invest, diversify, keep the money there, and watch it grow.

Common Passive Income Streams

1. Interest - This typically comes from a savings account, CD (Certificate of deposit), savings bonds, or stocks.
2. Dividends - Income earned from investments or partnerships.
3. Royalties - Income earned from products you sell or license.
4. Business income - This can only be passive if a system is built for the business that generates income without active work.
5. Rental income - Income earned from real estate.

Passive income ideas

1. *Certificate of Deposits (CD's):* Although, fairly low, this is one of the easiest and safest forms of passive income. CD's are an interest-paying savings option both short and long

term. You buy a CD and earn a fixed interest rate on your money. Earnings are typically two to three percent for 1-5 years. Bank minimums for CD's are typically $500; however, I have seen them for as low as $300.

2. *Stock Investment:* A stock is a share of ownership in a company. If one buys twenty Nike shares, you become part owner of Nike, a shareholder.

One easy way to get started is to invest in stocks that you like and/or support. More importantly, research to verify that the stock prices have a long history of steady growth over the life of the company. Make calculated investments. If a company has only been doing great for the last two years out of forty, you should probably pass on buying shares in that company.

We are living in a technological age, so be mindful of retail stocks. Many existing brick and mortar locations are closing because the boom of online purchasing has created lagging sales. Companies and stock investments continue to grow over time. This is a marathon not a sprint. You can open an investment account in person, or online and begin buying stock shares. Some examples of where you can open your investment accounts are Charles Schwab, Vanguard, Fidelity, and Robinhood (Allows you to buy a portion of a whole share, which can be very helpful if you are investing a set amount monthly).

3. *Stock Dividends:* The profit earned by a corporation is distributed as dividend to its shareholders. Most companies pay dividends quarterly; however, some pay semiannually or annually. Companies are not required to pay dividends. If dividends are something you are interested in research prior to determining stock purchases.

4. *Mutual Funds / Index funds:* This investment vehicle consists of a pool of money collected from many investors to invest in securities like stocks, bonds and other assets. Investing in mutual funds offers less risk through diversification. Diversification is a great option if you are unsure which single stock to buy. It can also reduce uncertainty of investing.

   The following index funds are strong examples of diversification within the stock market: Total Stock Market Index Fund, REIT Index Fund (Real Estate Investment Fund) and International Index Fund. The Total Stock Market Fund invests in 2,941 companies. Some of the top holdings being Apple and Amazon. REIT Index Funds are comprised of ninety-seven holdings, primarily office/industrial, residential and retail real estate. REITs have a smaller stake in storage, hotel and healthcare real estate. REITs provide dividends. The international fund invests in 2,144 medium and large companies outside of the United States such as Alibaba, Samsung and Toyota.

   Invest in these diverse funds with as little as one dollar. Mutual funds can be purchased through a brokerage account like Charles Schwab and Vanguard.

5. *Credit Card Rewards:* This unorthodox alternative is an easy way to earn passive income. This method can be worth hundreds, even thousands of dollars a year in cash, gift cards and travel. Many credit cards companies offer cash back on purchases between one and three percent. If you travel or would like to travel, you may opt to apply for an additional card that offers points for travel. Many of these cards will offer hefty 10,000 to 60,000 in bonus points and sometimes cash for travel redemption. Choose a card with no annual fee, if possible. There are plenty of options

out there. Create a separate banking account to track and transfer the cash from your primary bank account that was spent on the credit card. Use those funds to pay the credit card off in full prior to the statement closing date.

6. *Publish a book:* Kindle: It's never been easier to write a book and sell it on Amazon. Choose a price between $2.99 and $9.99 and earn a seventy percent royalty. Paperback: If you choose Kindle, it would make sense to offer the paper version with Amazon's print-on-demand services, or work directly with a distributor. No need to stockpile books in your garage. Audio: Some readers prefer to hear their books on audio. As a busy mom, I know I do.

7. *Sell digital files:* Sell images, photographs, quotes etc. Create it once or outsource the creation, upload and enjoy the passive income it creates. Use GIMP software (free), to create a digital image, digitize a hand drawn image or photo. GIMP is a cross-platform image editor. I created an Etsy store with unique images, where customers can purchase digital downloads. The platform is very user friendly. Etsy generates over three billion dollars in gross merchandise sales. The cost is nominal (Twenty cents per item listed, and five percent of the selling price), and the financial reward is limitless. Get some ideas from my store on Etsy, Beautifulyousf.

8. *Online Digital Courses:* Do you have expertise or know something that someone else could benefit from and would want to pay for? Create an online course. This is another great example of creating something once and making money over and over again. Use platforms such as Skillshare and Udemy if you don't have a large following.

9. *Sell Merchandise Online:* Create digital designs for t-shirts, leggings, hats, household items and more. Choose a third-party entity who does all of the work. Upload a design and/or message that appears on the item. The merchandise will be printed, packed and shipped. No need to store merchandise in your home. Zero upfront costs. Just sit back and collect the royalties. How wonderful! Who offers this? Companies who allow integration into online marketplaces. Printful and Zazzle.

10. *Rental Property/Real Estate:* Rent to a long-term tenant or use it as an Airbnb. Outsource management to a rental corporation or do it yourself. Don't own real estate? Find a rental unit in a popular location and create a contract with the owner to pay monthly rent and rent it out as an Airbnb, for profit.

11. *Sell Stock Photos, Music, Videos:* Do you love to create? This may be a great option for you. Sell photography, music or video clips. Create your work of art once and upload to the many online platforms available. I have purchased creative works from some of these sites. Shutterstock, iStock, Adobe stock and there are many more.

12. *Affiliate Marketing:* Do you have a website or use social media and have a good following? Affiliate marketing may be the passive income stream for you. Use Amazon Associates. It's absolutely free to sign up and very user friendly. Share products that you use and love, and if people buy using your link, you will be paid up to ten percent.

Why is passive income important?

Passive income is a wealth-building tool. It is the key to more time, financial independence and intergenerational wealth. Time is more important than money. It's the only commodity you cannot buy more of. Having more money affords you the ability to do what you truly enjoy in life – be able to eat the food you want, send children to any school you want, attend children's performances and school events, engage in hobbies you enjoy, live in the home you want, take the vacations you want, all when you want. Make money while you sleep so that you can do what you choose while awake.

Begin with one source of passive income. See it through to inception before you move to the next. Focus leads to growth. Things grow when attention is given. Creating consistent wins for yourself is key, no matter how small. Start with a passive income source that resonates most with you.

"She who makes $25,000 annually through passive income is more enviable than she who earns $100,000 annually through salary."

Mokokoma Mokhonoana

CHAPTER ELEVEN
THE $500 PLAN
PASSIVE INCOME MADE EASY.

"My favorite things in life don't cost any money. It's really clear that the most precious resource we have is time."

Steve Jobs

I AM SO excited to bring you this life-enriching challenge called, *The $500 Plan*! Manifest money and create savings in everyday life. The awesome part is that, *The $500 Plan* requires little to no self-sacrifice. The main purpose of this plan is to practice manifesting/creating money and saving towards a goal.

Manifest: When something is put into physical existence through thoughts, feelings, and beliefs.

The $500 Plan is a goal in which you save in $500 increments that will go toward your financial independence. Feel free to choose an amount that resonates best with you. Designate any amount that you feel is most attainable. You can always increase your goal if you feel you are reaching it with ease. The goal amount can be more or less than $500.

Where will the money come from to go toward, *The $500 Plan*?

This money will not come from your paycheck. The beauty is, it is coming from money that you create or manifest. Huh? How can I create money you ask? Easy, you already do it.

Anytime you create money in a nonconventional way: new freelance client, additional job, selling items in your home or closet, receiving unexpected discounts or free items. Those amounts would go toward, *The $500 Plan*.

Every time you make money (outside of a primary income source), save or find money, it will go into a separate savings account until you've reached your targeted goal. Once the goal is reached, invest it in a way that will create passive income, an investment toward long-term financial goals. The plan is simple – **Save $500. Invest. Repeat!**

More examples:

- When you go to the store to purchase a mirror that's advertised at $59, but when you arrive at the store, you find that the mirror has been reduced to $39. Cha-Ching! That's $20 that you manifested!

- Purchasing new shoes for your child. When you arrive at the store to make the purchase, the sales clerk lets you know that the store has a coupon that will save you twenty percent on your purchase. If the shoe's original cost is $50, you saved $10. Now you have ten dollars to deposit to, *The $500 Plan* account.

- Eating out with friends and someone is very insistent on paying or eating lunch with a friend and instead of bringing the bill the waiter says, that a kind gentleman a couple of tables over, already paid the tab. That's more money manifested. True, story.

- Receive an unexpected refund or check in the mail.

- If you have items in your home that you have purchased and have not used, you can even return them and put the money toward, *The $500 Plan.*

- Gather items around your home that you no longer wear or use and sell them.

- Speeding? You know that you were speeding, were pulled over and you didn't get a ticket. Congratulations! How much did you save? Put that in your account.

- Did you decide to skip your daily latte at the cafe? Add that amount to, *The $500 Plan.* Every single amount saved, counts.

The opportunities to create passive income are endless. *The $500 Plan* can be achieved in a passive way, like discounts, free stuff, unexpected checks, or take a more active role as a freelancer, get a second job, or sell unwanted items. The awesome part is whether you choose one or both routes, you will achieve your goal.

Use your manifested money as a down payment on your financial freedom. Pay off student loans, credit card bills, invest, save for a house etc. Another option is to use the cash as a money-making vehicle by starting your own business. Invest in something that will increase your income. Paying off debt is a way of increasing income because you will no longer be responsible for monthly finance fees, which is more money in your pocket.

The $500 Plan was created as an easy way to manifest money and save it! A goal without a plan is just a wish. Have fun with, *The $500 Plan.* Treat it like a game. Financial independence is your birthright. Become passionate about building passive income and create more time for yourself and your beautiful family. You can do it!

"Some people want it to happen. Some wish it would happen. Other's make it happen."

Michael Jordan

CHAPTER TWELVE
CREATE ADDITIONAL INCOME
USE YOUR FREE TIME TO FREE YOURSELF.

"I got my start by giving myself a start. Don't sit down and wait for the opportunities to come. Get up and make them."

Madame CJ Walker

WITH THE WORLD of online and social networks, creating additional income has never been easier. The world is yours!

Freelancer/Contractor:

Freelancing is working for multiple companies and/or individuals simultaneously as opposed to working for one single company. Freelancers take on contract work for companies and organizations. Do you have a valuable skill or service that you provide at your current employer, that you could offer as a freelancer? This could be a great option to get paid using your current skills outside of your current employer. Income varies.

Makeup Artist:

Are you naturally gifted at applying makeup? Women pay good money for this service. Use your face as your business card. Always leave home with fabulous makeup looks. When women tell you how beautiful you look, inform them that you are a makeup artist and offer them your card. Let friends and family know that you are selling your services as a professional makeup artist and to assist you in spreading the word. You could easily charge $20 - $40 for one makeup application. I have personally paid a makeup artist $30 to apply my makeup for a special event. Travel to clients or have them come to you.

Waitress/Bartender (high-end establishments):

A couple dining at a fine dining establishment can easily spend $300 to $1000 on one check. In some restaurants, even more. At fifteen percent, you could walk away with $45 - $150, and more, from one table. The same goes for bartending at an establishment where each drink is $20 and more. Many people drink as couples or groups, in which case, each individual will tend to have two or more alcoholic beverages. Upscale establishments preferred. Cha-ching!

Resale Items:

These could be items you own like personal gently-used clothing and accessories or unwanted household items. If you want to put in a little more time and effort, you can visit your local thrift shops, goodwill boutique, vintage stores or estate sales. Tip: thrift in wealthy neighborhoods in your area. I once purchased a Dolce and Gabbana blazer for $20. It was originally priced at $40, but since it had a small stain on the sleeve, the sales woman reduced the price in half. The retail value of the jacket was $700, and I sold it for $200. Now that was easy money. Use: Craigslist, eBay, Poshmark, etc. (for tips, see how I style my Poshmark store Beautiful@citygirlstyle)

Note: I tend to go for items that have a high probability to sell, and in a reasonable time frame. These items tend to be timeless, in style and preferably designer. Personally, I don't want to stockpile a bunch of items in my home. My goal is to turn the merchandise quickly. If it's sitting in my closet, it's not producing income and causing clutter. My goal is to have more income, not to own more stuff.

Social Media Manager:

Are you a social media wiz? Consider offering social media services to small businesses. This could be a tedious, laborious task that business owners may not have time to put effort into. You could start by approaching businesses that you frequent that have a great product, but little to no online presence. Grow their customer base by engaging the online community. Earn $20 - $35 per hour or determine a monthly rate.

Book Publicist:

It has never been easier to get a book published than it is today. Because publishing has become more easily accessible, many people are choosing this route. Whether someone selects self-publishing or traditional publisher, a book publicist is quite useful if you want to spread the word about your book through virtual book tours, book signings, interviews, speaking engagements, book reviews and ultimately sales. In the United States alone, over one million books are published annually, so there is a lot of competition. Publicist fees range from $2000 to $7000 per month or an hourly rate of $50-$80 an hour.

Audiobook Narrator:

You get to choose the books you want to audition for. There is an unlimited amount of opportunity to produce voice overs. Visit Acx.com. These are real audiobooks that will be available on Amazon, Audible and iTunes. Narrators can expect to earn on average $150 per finished book hour and approximately $1300 for a completed audiobook.

Real Estate Agent:

Be your own agent. Becoming a Real Estate agent is an especially great idea if you are in the market for purchasing a home. The sales commission on the sale of the house goes directly back to you. If within your personal network there is no Real Estate Agent, this leads you to more opportunity as well. Real Estate Agents earn anywhere between three to seven percent commission on the cost of the sale of the property. If you were to sell a house at a purchase price of $500,000 with a five percent commission fee, you would earn $25,000.

Exponential Growth of Time:

Use your time to generate money. Next, use the money to buy other people's time.

In this chapter I listed a few ways to create additional income. However, there are many more opportunities available depending on the city you live, skill level and income goals. Create additional income doing something you are passionate about or are skillful at. Think outside of the box. A few of my friends have offered desserts and dinners for sale and advertised on Facebook. They posted mouth-watering photos. Friends shared the information to their friends, and they sold out.

Multiple streams of income is always better than one. Money tends to gravitate to money and multiply.

> *"You can make more money being smart, than you can being strong or fast. The importance of developing intellectual property cannot be underestimated."*
>
> *Robert Smith*

CHAPTER THIRTEEN
EFFECTIVE NETWORKING
YOUR NETWORK IS YOUR NET WORTH.

"The richest people in the world look for and build networks, everyone else looks for work. Marinate on that for a minute."

Unknown.

HAVE YOU EVER heard the saying, "Your network is your net worth?" This is especially true of freelance work and business opportunities. Growing your network will make growing your additional income source so much more lucrative. Attend events and make genuine connections. Don't merely go through the robotic motions that many do when trying to drum up business, simply trying to sell themselves and pass out as many business cards as possible. That does not get you business. If you attend events regularly, you will begin to see many of the same individuals, and through those repeat interactions, that is how genuine connections are made. Set a goal for yourself as to how often you would like to go out to network. My goal is once a week, sometimes I'm able to attend more events. Choose a goal that you can commit to. Of course, if you exceed the goal you set for yourself, that's awesome!

Networking:

The most effective way to network is to look at it as a social interaction versus, "Buy my product. Buy my service." No one likes to be sold. Bring the characteristics of the "Pleasing Personality" in chapter five, and you've got this! The possibilities are endless. Choose events that will put you outside of your comfort zone. The potential outside of your comfort zone is limitless. I highly suggest joining at least one club or organization that meets regularly. This is an excellent way to grow your network and get practice, as you will have the same people attending regular meetings.

Many networking opportunities are single-mom friendly. When I attended merchant meetings, volunteer meetings and most meetings for that matter, I brought my brother and daughter at any age. I made sure I brought lots of snacks, coloring books, quiet toys – anything engaging. If meetings were long, I would allow a thirty to forty-five-minute educational show on my computer. If your child is school aged, homework is another option.

Clubs/Organization:

Chamber of Commerce

Join your local Chamber of Commerce. Attend monthly meetings and become aware of business opportunities in your city. You may also choose to join the Chamber of Commerce that focuses on ethnic backgrounds. For example: African American, Asian American, Hispanic, French, etc.

Local Merchants Association

Neighborhoods within a city will often have a local merchant's group. You do not have to be a current business owner to join this group. Typically, they meet monthly to discuss business opportunities, programs and sometimes a speaker that will present to the group.

Meetup

Meetup.com has an endless amount of groups within areas of interest. There is truly something for everyone. Groups usually have one or more meet-ups per month. What's great about Meetup.com is that you are free to attend however many or few events you want. I experienced great benefits from a golf group, business group and women's social group. Free to join.

Book Club

Local book clubs usually meet once a month and talk about a book that was designated one month prior. What's great is if you don't have time to sit down and read, you can listen to the audio version. What I love about joining a book club is that you meet new people and enrich your mind at the same time. Win. Win.

Wine Club

Growing your knowledge of wine and meeting new people is another excellent option. If you are a creature of habit like me, what I love about this option is that the group visits different wineries/wine establishments monthly. I have had the opportunity to visit beautiful establishments right in my own city that I never knew existed and meet some awesome people in the process.

Toastmasters

Meet regularly to improve vocabulary, speaking, leadership, communication skills and ultimately confidence. Many of the attendees are business professionals looking to grow their leadership and presentation skills. Engaging with people who are actively working on self-improvement is always a plus. They have locations around the globe and it's free to join.

Volunteer

Volunteering is both enriching and rewarding. Choose an area of interest that you are passionate about. Volunteer for a one-time event or longer term for an individual organization or non-profit. I once had a friend who volunteered as an usher at Les Brown's event. She had the opportunity to meet the famed motivational speaker in person.

Want a longer-term role? Many non-profit organizations are always happy to have more help. While volunteering at events, you usually attend for free.

Go it alone:

It is understandable to want to attend events with friends. It's comfortable! The issue is, friends may not be on the same path as you. I challenge you to challenge yourself, to attend events solo. I promise, you will meet people. Some of my best connections and opportunities were made when I attended events solo. If you must go with a friend, divide and conquer. Don't stick by each other's side during the majority of the event. The objective is to meet "new" people, and that is more difficult to do if the majority of your time is occupied by someone you already know. Remember, nothing grows inside of your comfort zone. We all came into this world alone and will leave alone, so let's get more comfortable with ourselves.

Socializing/Networking Events:

Events do not need to be classified as "networking event" in order for you to meet more people to expand your social/ business network. The key is to increase the amount of people you know, and make connections. I love to mix business and pleasure by attending events that I enjoy, socializing with new people, and welcoming opportunities. I firmly believe the experience should be both engaging and enriching but also be fun. Use Eventbrite, Funcheap, or Google-specified events in your area and choose what makes sense. Some ideas are book signings/author talks, galas, fundraisers, community events, holiday parties, plays, and jazz performances. The opportunities are endless. If you choose to indulge in alcohol at the events, drink responsibly. The ultimate goal is to socialize and network coherently.

Begin growing your network now, even if you are unsure which secondary revenue source is for you. It's better to be growing your personal network so you have some connections while you determine what your additional revenue source will be. Additionally, you can help others by sending business, opportunities, or beneficial information their way. When you are open to assisting others without expecting anything in return, you will find that people will be drawn to help you. It is the great power of generosity.

"I've learned that people will forget what you said, people will forget what you did, but people will never forget how you made them feel."

Maya Angelou

CHAPTER FOURTEEN
THE POWER OF GENEROSITY

"The best way to find yourself is to lose yourself in the service of others."

Mahatma Gandhi

GENEROSITY: SHOWING OR having a readiness to give more of something, such as time, money, or kindness. Giving more than is necessary or expected.

Generosity is magnetic. Not only does the receiver benefit, the giver obtains intrinsic value much greater than money. Whether generosity comes in the form of time, money, or simple pleasantries, even the simplest acts of kindness can have a massive impact on the receiver's day or even life.

A baby will die if not held. It has been clinically proven that adults are not all that different. According to nbcnews.com, "A review of 148 studies concluded that on average, having stronger social ties increased likelihood of an individual's overall survival by as much as 50 percent." Humans are social animals. We cannot thrive in the world without one another. It is not enough to live in this life and only consume. One cannot truly live an abundant life without generosity. Give to someone outside of yourself to live a truly rich life.

Begin your journey of generosity by choosing an area you have an interest or passion. Not every person has the capacity to give of oneself entirely like Malcolm X or Mother Theresa. As much as I would love to build a school for girls, in Africa, I don't possess the financial resources of Oprah Winfrey. The point I am trying to make is that it is okay to begin your journey of generosity right where you are right now. What is most important is to begin.

6 Easy Ways to Become a More Generous Person

1. **Donate:** Choose to donate to an organization whose cause you believe in. Often schools ask for donations. It totally counts if you donate to your children's school. This amount can be anything you want, literally. If $5 or $25 is all that you have to give, give that. There will come a time when you can give more, and you will. Donations are supposed to come from the heart, so it truly is the thought that counts.

2. **Pay it Forward:** Brighten someone's day by giving the cashier additional money to pay for something of your choosing. Give the gift of coffee, flowers, bridge toll etc. Let the cashier know that the next person's coffee, toll or dozen roses are courtesy of you, just because. This is a fun way to give that is truly selfless because often, the person you blessed will not have the opportunity to thank you because in most cases you would have already left. Hopefully, the people you surprise will do the same for someone else, and so on.

3. **Charity Events:** I have had the opportunity to attend some really fun charity events, and the cost ranges vastly. Whether you attend a Spaghetti Feed at a school for $20 per person or a gala that costs $500, there is something for everyone and so many options in between.

4. **Conversation:** Have you ever come across a person, be it a senior, child, or anyone who craved acknowledgment or wanted to talk. You may only have time for a smile and hello and that's great. However, there will be times when you have a few additional moments to spare. Treat others how you want to be treated. Do you want to be treated like a V.I.P. or peasant? It helps to maintain the mindset that you will treat everyone you come in contact with as if they were the CEO of a Fortune 500 company for which you want to be hired. You would unlikely brush them off with a half-hearted glance. The moral of the story is to treat all people well. Kindness is free, and you have the opportunity to be sunshine in someone's cloudy day.

5. **Collect Litter:** Take a short walk, five minutes or more. This could be on your break while working, before, after work, or anytime in between. Bring gloves and a bag to collect garbage you see on the street. Get some exercise while cleaning up the planet.

6. **Volunteer:** Giving your time can be one of the most generous gestures you can donate. Time is the most precious commodity that we have in life. Why? Time is irreplaceable. You cannot earn or buy more. We all have a finite amount of time in this life. There is an infinite amount of things you can do to be generous with time. Be a blessing to someone in your life. Volunteering, can be as simple as helping a friend or relative out. There are also a number of places within your city that you can volunteer. Start by choosing an area of interest then search online. You can also volunteer at your child's school. Who better to reap the benefits of your generosity than your own children. Schools and classrooms typically have many duties they need help with. I have had the opportunity to volunteer as a room parent, and at various events the school

offers for students and families. It shows teachers and staff that you are committed to your child and the school. I have built lasting relationships with parents and teachers while staying connected to the community. Win. Win.

You can also choose to volunteer at local community groups (non-profits) who typically meet once a month for two hours. I had the good fortune to meet great people while being educated as to what was happening in the community, like free/low cost programming for children and adults. I learned about job and grant opportunities through meeting prominent figures within the community. By volunteering my time, I was able to gain opportunities for my child and myself that I otherwise would not have had.

6 Reasons Why You Should Become More Generous

1. **Benefits of generosity.** Generosity is known to make you happier, healthier, and increase satisfaction in life. A five-year, multi-institutional study performed by Michael J. Poulin, Ph.D., assistant professor of psychology, at the University at Buffalo, discovered that giving, thus being generous, not only helps the receiver, but it can also provide protection of health and prolong the life of the giver. The study also found that the giver and receiver both reaped similar benefits.

2. **Generosity Reduces Stress.** Can money buy happiness? In this case, it certainly can. Elizabeth W. Dunn, Laura B. Aknin of the University of British Columbia and Michael I. Norton of Harvard Business School performed a study that found that spending money on others promotes happiness while purchasing consumer goods for oneself did not offer lasting happiness. After performing multiple spending

tests with volunteers, the study's findings suggested that spending as little as $5 on someone else, may be sufficient to provide increased happiness. We know that stress causes cortisol levels to rise. There have been links between stress and disease. Over time, raised levels of cortisol causes stress and wear on the body, which can result in premature aging, mental health challenges, and disease. As single moms, we can take all of the happiness boosts available. And for a mere $5, I'll take a smoothie with a side of happiness boost, please!

3. **Generosity Helps Release Endorphins.** Endorphins are known as the happy hormone which, when released, gives feelings of euphoria and general wellness. Generosity is good for your health. Doing good things for others promotes endorphin release. According to medical sources, endorphins produce positive feelings in the body, quite similar to morphine. Remember as young school-aged children, everyone volunteered to hand out papers or erase the chalkboard for the teacher. As a kid, I felt extra happy when I got the opportunity to help the teacher, and now it's clear why.

4. **Longer Richer Life.** Research has shown that generosity greatly improves the immune system and lengthens lifespan.

5. **Accept Generosity.** As single mothers, we are not only the givers of life but pretty much everything else. However, it is essential to be accepting of others' generosity toward us. Being overly independent takes away the joy that loved ones feel when they are giving. Generosity is an act of love and kindness that you are beyond deserving of. Never say things like, "I don't deserve this," or "This is too much." Instead, show gratitude by saying, "Thank you!" This is the

perfect opportunity to accept with open arms and count your blessings.

6. **Attitude of Gratitude.** Embrace your life right now, and be thankful for your life and all of its intricacies. Use a notebook or journal to keep track of your daily blessings. Make a list of what you are grateful for. The list can be as short or as long as you would like. My list always includes my family, our great health, and the roof we have over our heads. Sit in silence for just a few minutes, and think about what you wrote. As you sit, feel thankful, and allow your mind, body, and soul to be filled with gratitude. Finding gratitude in life's challenges is a bonus.

Generosity is more than being able to give, but the ability to receive graciously, so the giver can also benefit from the exchange. Focus on giving that produces a positive effect on the receiver. Generosity is meant to improve the wellbeing of individual/s to whom it contributes. Give thoughtfully and purposefully.

> *"If you look at what you have in life, you'll always have more. If you look at what you don't have in life, you'll never have enough."*
>
> *Oprah Winfrey*

CHAPTER FIFTEEN
TECH-SAVVY MOM
PUTTING KIDS FIRST.

"Technology is a useful servant but a dangerous master."
~ Unknown.

LIVING IN THE technological age with so many distractions, and instant gratification being a go to for many, being mindful how these things can change our state of mind is imperative. Be aware of time stealers such as social media, television, electronic devices, and even the telephone. Do not allow technology to steal our time and patience from our children.

Have you ever found yourself scrolling through your phone whether it was looking at your email or scrolling through social media, and your child tries to get your attention? How do you respond? I can attest to having been short and impatient in my response if I gave one at all. I was like a robot. So focused on my device, I did not give my child the time and patience they deserved. How many people do you see on public transportation, in restaurants, at the park, even walking down the street looking mindlessly at their devices?

Based on research from author and Clinical Psychologist Catherine Steiner-Adair, she concludes that, "When you're texting or answering emails, the part of your brain that is engaged in the 'to do' part, where there's also a sense of urgency to get the task accomplished, a sense of time pressure. So, we're much more irritable when interrupted." Stein-Adair interviewed 1000 children between the ages of four and eighteen, asking about their parents' use of mobile devices. The language that repeatedly came up was "sad, mad, angry, and lonely." A four-year-old interviewee called his dad's smartphone a "stupid phone." Some children recalled cheerfully throwing their parent's phone into the toilet, hiding it in the oven or other naughty places. Another child's reply was, "I feel like I'm just boring. I'm boring my dad because he will take any text, any call, anytime-even on the ski lift!" Straight from the mouth of children. Electronic devices have enormous control of our attention, concentration and lives.

My own child once has asked, "Mom can you please get off of the phone and talk to me?" This happened after I had picked her up from school one day. Wow! If we think about it, if a friend were in the car or visiting with us would we so rudely be engrossed in our devices? The answer is likely no, so why do that to our kids?

Never in a million years would I want my daughter to think she was unimportant or boring. Communication is key. I know it would be unrealistic to never use phones or devices in the presence of your children. Placing perimeters that work for you around your device usage while you are parenting will make your children feel more valued. Be sure to inform your children of those limits you have set for yourself. I informed my daughter that I would only take very important calls while she is riding with me; all others can wait. Now, she knows that she matters.

Children are very smart and resilient. They understand that Mommy has to work and/or has other responsibilities. Communication is key. I limit my phone calls in general when we are together. About ninety percent of the calls I do not take. So, I may take about ten percent of the calls, and five percent of those are fairly brief. Now I am able to utilize our car rides and time, in general, to have meaningful conversations and build a bond stronger than ever.

Concerning computer usage, getting up early in the morning, or staying up at night while the kiddos are sleeping is an option. For me, quality time is so important. After all, if I wanted more sleep, I would have passed on motherhood. If your children have homework you can work while they're working. This does not always necessarily work out because sometimes they may need help, which could often be the case. Quiet time is always an option. This is when you give your child something to do by themselves quietly, whether that's to read a book, draw, color, put together a puzzle, etc. This is a great alternative because you can work alongside your child, where you are both doing something constructive and meaningful. I did not suggest television, iPad or computer because chances are, if children are school age, they are working on electronic devices often, and so personally, unless it's something educational, this option would be rare. The average child will sit in front of an electronic device for hours with no problem. When my child is watching a movie, her mind won't even register hunger. Unless it's educational, I call it mindless television. All too often, our children are watching too much of it, picking up not so positive behaviors or language as a result. Social media is no better. Screens are highly stimulating and addictive, and I strongly recommend limiting daily screen usage and setting parameters around device usage.

Infants and toddlers require tons of time—no way around that. More often than not, your time for electronics will be during nap time. Fortunately, most infants take lots of naps. However, you may need that time to sleep also.

Keep in mind that while working alongside your child, you are likely not to be nearly as productive as if you were working alone. So please, lower your expectations to avoid disappointment. More than anything, you're building a bond. Your child(ren) will feel proud, "I'm working with Mommy," or "I'm working like Mom." Be it consciously or subconsciously. Plant positive seeds that will grow with time.

As tech-savvy moms who put kids first, let's be sure they continue to feel important and loved. Set electronic boundaries for yourself and children. Model healthy electronic usage. Set electronic free zones like meals, bedtime and car rides. Quality time spent bonding is more important than mere time spent in each other's presence.

"Time has a wonderful way of showing us what really matters."

Unknown.

CHAPTER SIXTEEN
MOMMY MAGIC
THE PATH TO SUCCESSFUL PARENTING.

"My mother is my root, my foundation. She planted the seed that I base my life on, and that is the belief that the ability to achieve starts in your mind."

Michael Jordan

MAGIC: TO CREATE, transform, move. . . as if by magic. The power of influencing.

Cheer: encouragement, comfort, approval, vocal supporter.

Leader: Someone who leads. The ability to bring out the best in people.

Children look up to their mothers. Being the very first point of contact to the world, we possess an innate bond that is like no other. Speak life into your children. Tell them who you want them to be with your actions. Be the best role model you can be. Kids look to their moms for love, encouragement, self-assurance, and leadership. This will aid in building self-esteem and a strong sense of self that will be the foundation for their positive emotional and mental well-being.

We want as much as humanly possible to always be speaking to our kids with love and kindness. One of our goals as parents is that as adults, our children have the ability to look back on their childhood fondly. Kids are brilliant, and as they grow they know who is there, supporting them emotionally and financially. The most important thing is that our children grow up feeling loved, supported, and cared for. Moms are the best cheerleaders.

How to Best Support Our Children:

1. Be their biggest cheerleader. You can do it! I'm so proud of how hard you try. You are intelligent. You are kind and thoughtful. You can accomplish whatever you put your mind to, etc.

2. Show up to support activities, academic programs or accolades in school. Send a relative or close friend if you just can't make it. Have someone videotape the activities so that you can later watch it with your child.

3. Spend quality time together especially at dinner and breakfast. (without electronics)

4. Take a vested interest in your child's likes and desires. Even something as simple as giving them your undivided attention as they recite a speech, multiple times, that they've spent hours working on.

5. Most Importantly. Don't be over critical of your child. They are new at life and learning. We have an imperative role as moms to support, direct, and teach, all with love.

The Rose and the Thorn

Life can be filled with ups and downs, positives and negatives, roses and thorns, of which we have no control. However, what we do have mastery of is our reaction and how we choose to allow these moments to affect us. Each day, whether on the car ride home, or at the dinner table, begin asking your child to tell you about one rose and one thorn in their day. The rose is one great thing, and the thorn is one not so great occurrence that transpired during the day.

Some children's rose examples may be; I played my favorite game during recess, we had ice cream during snack or I got an A on a test. Listen with open ears, enthusiasm, and express how happy you are to hear it. Thorn examples may be; my best friend did not want to play with me, I didn't get to play with my favorite toy, or I got a D on a test. Learn from thorns by turning them into teachable moments. Ask your child how they could turn the thorn into a rose or how they could have improved the situation at that moment. Assist your child by aiding in cultivating their answer. Younger children will need more assistance at first.

For example, if a close friend chooses not to play with your child, ask clarifying questions to find out what happened. Ask how it made your child feel. Validate their feelings and encourage them by saying something like, "We all have bad days. As kids sometimes the smallest things can be upsetting. The good news is you are so lucky to have many more friends that adore you to play with. I'm sure Tanya will come around." Suppose the child received a low score on a test. Reassure your child that they are brilliant, and unfortunately, tests don't always reflect that. Ask if they studied to the best of their abilities. If not, let them know it's great that they realize they could have studied more, and next time, you're sure they will. Tell your child you are there to help if they need it. If they put in proper preparation for the test, present them with other options they may consider like, asking for extra credit or completing test corrections for additional credit.

There is almost always a way to turn thorns into roses. The point of this exercise is to 1.) Engage with your child and find out what went well and not so well in their day. 2). Give attention and show interest in their daily lives. 3.) Give advice on how to cope with moments in life that are not perfect or ideal. Some days your child will have no thorns, which is excellent. Teach your children how to celebrate positive moments in life and turn lemons into apple juice. Make the impossible, possible. Shift a negative experience into a positive one. Share your rose's and thorn's too! This exercise is a great lesson in confronting failure and disappointment, problem solving, effective communication, positive self-image, and optimism for children.

Rock Star Parenting: Moms are far from perfect. We may assume our parenting skills are on point; however, our children may be thinking and feeling differently. How do you find out the truth? Check-in with each child individually and separately to ask, "How am I doing as a Mom?" If you were to rate me between 1 and 10, 1 being not so good and 10 being amazing, you are killing it! What number would you give me?" Important: Whatever the score your child gives, do not get mad, or judge them negatively. Remain neutral and most importantly, remain open. The next question is, "How can I get to a 10?" The point of the question is to do better. If we know better we can do better. Getting down to the root of what your child feels is the goal, and then to give them what they need.

Remember, this exercise has less to do with material items and more to do with feeding the child's soul, well-being, and contributing to their growth in a positive, uplifting way. We can give our children all of the material items in the world but what they need and want most is love and us! Even if they don't realize it.

Example: A child gives a seven because they did not get the new LeBron James, shoes he/she wanted or didn't get to go on a Hawaiian 5-star holiday in the summer. We want to validate their feelings because we do not know how they may feel inside. If your child's answer is similar to this one, where you receive a lower score because they did not get non-essential material items, ask them if you provided the thing they wanted would that make you a better mom. Talk it out and most importantly, listen.

Mom's perception of parenting performance, versus what children are feeling could be completely off. This exercise gives us room to grow and improve. I like to check in every 3 - 4 months. I learned this awesome parenting tip from the famed author and speaker, Lisa Nichols.

Mommy magic is evident. A mother's influence is one of the most powerful miracles in the world. We have a massive impact on future generations. The importance of being a supportive, loving mom is paramount to our children's physical and mental well-being. Ongoing dialog, and interactive exercises like the ones above, reinforce communication, self-esteem, positive behavior, teach problem-solving and build strong bonds. Moms are the most remarkable beings on the planet. There is no limit to what we can do. Give your child a hug if by chance you need a reminder of how magical you are.

"Leadership is not a position or a title, it is action and example."

Unknown.

CHAPTER SEVENTEEN
IT'S ALL ABOUT ME, TIME!
PRIORITIZE AND REVITALIZE.

"Amazing health is true wealth!"

Takiyah

"I have learned that it is no one else's job to take care of me but me."

Beyonce

ALL ABOUT ME, Time!

Kids time, work time, family time, chore time. Lastly, and if it even makes it to the list, ME time. As single mothers that are doing it all on our own, let's face it, our work is rarely ever done. We take on many different unpaid professions, because frankly if we don't do it, no one else will. Those professions include but are not limited to: Chef (and I say chef instead of cook because all of the newfound finicky appetites of children today. You must be notches above a cook to get them to eat anything nowadays.), tutor (in all subjects), doctor, RN, specialist, nanny, taxi cab driver, maid, playmate, cheerleader, coach, life coach, manager and contractor. If you have more than one child, add referee. We even take on full-on character personalities. Let's not forget the Tooth Fairy, the Easter Bunny, and Santa.

At the end of the day, we *love* our children. No Regrets. Bringing life into the world is a very special and rare gift. A miracle! Nothing else is more amazing. At the same time, if we're honest with ourselves, we know that kids can suck the life out of you. Every ounce. They can even turn you into the Tasmanian Devil! I digress. To be the best mom for our children we have to recharge our battery. Let me emphasize, recharge. If at all possible, away from your kids. A healthy balance is important. In this chapter, I'm going to show you some ways to be a little bit selfish. Everyone else gets time, so why shouldn't you?

Let's raise a glass. This section is all about us, to ME time. Cheers!

Mommy Time Out

A moment, a breather, brief solitude, self-reflection. That's right; Mommy needs a time-out. Baby is wailing because of teething, the toddler is launching meatballs across the room, the kindergartener is arguing over a toy, the preteen is having a mental meltdown about homework, and the teenager is complaining about not being able to go away on holiday like her friends. Let's throw in sleep deprivation for good measure. Any of these, sound familiar? Just makes you want to crawl under a rock and hide. And you should, hence Mommy time-out.

First, take a long deep breath. When chaos is amiss it can cause us to think unclearly. If you have small children, it is important first to make sure they are safe and secure so they will not injure themselves. Some ideas are a baby bed, playpen, swing etc. It's also important that you are not cooking or have any sharp, unsafe objects lying around. Be smart. If your kids are old enough to understand, simply tell them, "I need a moment. I will be back to help you in a few minutes." Once the kids are safe, it's time to run for cover. Now, this is a time out, so it should be brief, five minutes or less. What it does is allow time to diminish stress and regroup.

Mommy's time-out is simply a well-deserved break. Below are some additional ideas:

- Lock yourself in a room (bathroom, bedroom, etc.).
- Look in the mirror and tell yourself how amazing and patient you are.
- Wash your face.
- Pray for strength, patience, and peace.
- Meditate. Think of something that makes you insanely happy.
- Recite positive affirmations.
- Count to ten slowly while breathing deeply.
- Play your favorite song
- Dance.
- Stretch.
- Make a cup of relaxing tea (chamomile).
- Drink a glass of wine.
- Count your blessings.

Need more time? One alternative would be to hire a sitter/ mother helper to allow yourself some free time. Perhaps two hours per week, or whatever is doable for you and your budget. There's always childcare trades with a friend. Be creative.

4 Not-so-apparent indicators that Mommy needs a time-out.

- Complaining or fussing at your children more than you are loving and praising them.
- Getting frustrated with your children for minuscule things that don't matter.

- Instead of listening to your children, you only tell them what to do.
- Judging your children, often based on past experiences.

Drink Wine Unapologetically

Look. I'm not saying guzzle wine until you fall into a drunken haze. But let's face it, for some, wine can be survival. So, if I have to choose between screaming at the kids because they are misbehaving or drinking wine and calmly diffusing the situation like a Buddhist Monk, I'm choosing the Buddhist Monk. Sometimes wine equals sanity. I am a firm believer in moderation. Be responsible, of course. Even Jesus turned water into wine. He must have been thinking of the single Mom. Amen.

Red wine can be good for your health. "Red wine contains antioxidants, particularly polyphenols provided by the grapes," says Gabby Greerts, Registered Dietitian. "Polyphenols have been shown to improve heart function and blood pressure, thus reducing the risk of cardiovascular disease." Up to five ounces. Harvard professor David Sinclair, PhD., has found evidence that resveratrol, an active ingredient in red wine can slow down the aging of cells, which translates into slowing down the aging of our bodies.

For moms who don't drink wine, your strength is admirable. Stay with your principles. I love a great cup of herbal tea, which is also packed full of health benefits. Green tea is my drink of choice, and it has more caffeine than coffee. When I have my tea as a means of relaxation, you would think I was being served at The Ritz. Be over the top, make your experience the best. You deserve it! Be sure to get all of your necessities. Start with a tray and your favorite tea, a cloth napkin with a ring, cup and saucer. I highly recommend a lit candle. Something that smells divine and puts you on cloud nine. If you have flowers, add them to your tray, even the artificial ones create a beautiful ambiance. Add a picture frame with an inspirational quote or a beautiful scene. Prepare your favorite tea with fresh lemon and raw sugar. If you really want to be fancy make some triangle-shaped sandwiches or add a dessert. This is all, of course a guideline. Customize to recreate your own Ritz-like experience. Go ahead, spoil you!

Try Something New. Go it Alone if you have to.

We live in a society where complacency is the norm. Living inside of the box can be a place of comfort for many. But I promise you, when you color outside of the lines, you'll feel a sense of self-satisfaction and accomplishment.

After parenting, feeding, changing, working, driving to and from kids activities, and helping with homework, we just want to plop on our beds and go to sleep. When the kids are away from home, and we have free time, sleeping and vegging out can be like a slice of heaven. No one to care for but yourself, even if it's for just a few hours. Nirvana! I like to gather some of my favorite foods, a nice book or watch a good movie and RELAX. You definitely need those days too. Love them!

Glamming up and going out may be the furthest idea from your mind. However, I implore you to do so as often as possible. Being a woman is harder than being a man. Let's just state the obvious. There is a list of dutiful maintenance women endure daily, weekly and monthly. Women are amazing, beautiful creatures. We give life and multitask! Enough said. So maybe I'm a little biased, but when I look at a single mom I think, "Wow! Wonder Woman in the flesh." Frankly, mothers in general. While Wonder Woman was out fighting crime and saving the world, she looked put together doing it. I know what you're thinking, and I'm well aware that Wonder Woman is a fictional character on television. But we are mothers, the cornerstone of society, Princesses, Queen's, and Life-givers. When we put time and effort into ourselves, we radiate. We look better and thus feel better. So let's fix the hair, and give the workout gear (as a wardrobe) a much-needed rest. It's easy to take on the peasant role and place ourselves last on every single list. No more I say. It's time to try something new. Give it a try. You're guaranteed to feel better.

Stepping out!

There are tons of things to do in your city; you just have to seek them out. The options can be limitless, ranging from free to expensive. Explore Eventbrite, Fun Cheap and Groupon.

Fun "Leveled Up" activities to engage in.

- Day party
- Fundraiser/Gala (have fun and give back)
- Book Signing/Author Discussion
- Art Gallery
- Join a book club or Start one
- Join a wine club
- Wine tasting
- Play/Theatre
- Community Events (often free or low cost)
- Live Band/Music/Performance
- Ballet
- Opera
- Workshop/class
- Small Business Week (in your city or nearby city)
- Dance class

- Exercise of choice
- Driving range/Golf
- Sporting events (Professional or College)
- Sightseeing Bus Tour (In your own city or nearby city)
- Paint Night
- Day Spa
- Day or evening boat cruise
- Comedy show
- Festivals

Go out with friends, or go alone and make new ones!

Not quite ready to go it alone. Join a meet-up group to meet new people. Do something you've never done or do something you love. Try meetup.com

What tends to happen when you are in a group?

Safe. Safety net. Comfort.

We tend to stay in our safety net which is our friend. Comfy and easy, yes! But, it's only when we venture out alone that we allow ourselves to be more open to meeting new people. It takes us out of our area of comfort better known as a comfort zone.

Me time is an absolute necessity, not an indulgence. Prioritizing everyone's care before your own does not make you a better mom. A more tired, worn-down mom, perhaps. While it's not essential to be first on the care list, moms need to be at the top. When moms are relaxed and calm, parenting becomes more effortless. Taking time to love and pour back into your own well-being and to de-stress allows for a greater ability to have interactions with children that are filled with patience and love. The mind, body, and soul of a mom, needs to be nurtured, just as children are. Modeling healthy, self-love and care is a beautiful gift that you can pass down to your children.

Ultimately, if you don't consider yourself a priority, how do you expect anyone else to.

> *"When you take care of yourself, you're a better person for others. When you feel good about yourself, you treat others better."*
>
> Solange Knowles

CHAPTER EIGHTEEN
EPILOGUE

"I'm not really single. I mean, I am, but I have a son. Being a single mother is different from being a single woman."

Kate Hudson.

SINGLE MOTHERHOOD IS a journey full of growth and opportunity. It's not always easy but, anything worth having rarely comes easily. We are never given more than we can bear. Find the lessons in your challenges as well as in your victories. Grow and become an even better version of yourself.

Being a single mother can often mean twice the work. However, the beautiful outcome is that you receive two times the reward. Your children will love, adore, praise, support, and be there for you. They see your selfless efforts. Perfection is an allusion, instead strive for excellence in all that you do. When moms are doing their best, children recognize that. Be kind to yourself. It's impossible to do better than YOUR best.

Children are wonderful little beings and gifts not only to us as moms, but to the world. Notice how people light up at the sight of a baby, and wave when they see a toddler teetering about or interact inquisitively with a teenager. Children are born without fear and a curiosity for life. Many adults often lose these characteristics because we have been programmed to be fearful. "Don't do that," "Don't touch that," "No!" "Be quiet," Be still," "You can't," "That's impossible." The good news is that we can reprogram ourselves through choice, habits, and repetition. Foster optimism and courage in your kids. It is our job as parents to cultivate curiosity by creating an environment filled with love, happiness, and support. It really begins with us. Children are often a mirror image of what they observe and experience. Become the best version of yourself and embody the reflection you want to see in your children. The tools are here, and it truly is that simple.

Life is a beautiful gift, given to us by way of sight, sound, scent, passion and love. The same is true of concepts - guidance, rich ideals and sincerity, like the compelling ideas this book has provided. What will you do with it? Give it away! As we learned from "Chapter Fourteen" on "Generosity", giving to others will benefit the receiver and you. Send a copy of this book to mom's you know, NEED IT. You can change someone's life.

The life that you create for yourself begins and ends with you. Being a mom is both a gift and a blessing. You are the chosen one. Wear the title of mom like a crown and rule your kingdom as such. I salute you.

"Yes, I do have a big ego. . .and I am in love with myself. . .Because if you don't love yourself, how can anybody love you back?"

Mel B

THANK YOU

DEAR AMAZING MOMS,

Many thanks for using your most precious resource, time, to support this book. As a token of my gratitude, I have given you a list of resources that will aid you on your motherhood journey.

Moms always want the best for their children so here's a trick. Should you decide to bless the world with more children, and/or upon choosing another mate, ask yourself, would you want your daughter to date that person? Or, would you be happy and proud if your son turned out like your potential partner?

Be well and prosper.

Love,

Single Mom And The City

P.S. We're Social! Join us City Mom's on Instagram at, therealsinglemomandthecity and the private Facebook group, Single Mom And The City. Full of positive vibes. See you there!

RESOURCES

Suggested Reading

The Wealth Choice	Author: Dr. Dennis Kimbro
Think and Grow Rich	Author: Napoleon Hill
The Alchemist	Author: Paulo Coalo
Talent is Overrated	Author Geoff Colvin
How Children Succeed	Author: Paul Tough
The Deepest Well	Author: Dr. Nadine Burke Harris (Surgeon General of California)

YouTube Channel Recommendations

Infinite Waters (Change Your Life! Awaken Your Infinite Power.)

Lewis Howes (The School of Greatness)

Our Rich Journey (Financial Independence - Save. Earn. Invest.)

Dr. Boyce Watkins (Financial Channel)

Heal Your Living (Mindfulness. Sustainability. Minimalism. Wellness.)

At Home With Nikki (Home Organization Tips)

Rachel Ama (Easy Healthy Vegan Recipes)

Unclaimed Property - California State Controller's Office
https://www.sco.ca.gov/upd_msg.html

REFERENCES

ABC News. (2006). Tyra Banks Experiences Obesity Through Fat Suit. *ABC News*. Retrieved from https://abcnews.go.com/ GMA/BeautySecrets/story?id=1280787

Adam, H., & Galinsky, A. (2012). Enclothed cognition. *Journal of Experimental Social Psychology*, *48*(4), 918-925. doi: 10.1016/j.jesp.2012.02.008

Babcock, L., Laschever, S., Small, D., & Gelfand, M. (2003). Nice Girls Don't Ask. Retrieved 23 August 2020, from https://hbr.org/2003/10/nice-girls-dont-ask

Birdthistle, W., & Hemel, D. (2018). The 401(k) Is Turning 40 Years Old. It's Past Time We Change How Americans Save for Retirement. Retrieved 23 August 2020, from https://time.com/5440542/401k-retirement/

Chu, M. (2017). Research Reveals That Publicly Announcing Your Goals Makes You Less Likely to Achieve Them. Retrieved 23 August 2020, from https://www.inc.com/ melissa-chu/announcing-your-goals-makes-you-less-likely-to-ach.html#:~:text=Productivity-,Research%20 Reveals%20That%20Publicly%20Announcing%20Your%20 Goals,Less%20Likely%20to%20Achieve%20Them

Coyle, D. (2017). How Being Happy Makes You Healthier. Retrieved 23 August 2020, from https://www.healthline.com/ nutrition/happiness-and-health#TOC_TITLE_HDR_3

Cromie, W. (2003). Wine molecule slows aging process: Scientists drink to that. *The Harvard Gazette*. Retrieved from https://news.harvard.edu/gazette/story/2003/09/ wine-molecule-slows-aging-process-/

Dunn, E., Aknin, L., & Norton, M. (2008). Spending Money on Others Promotes Happiness. *Science, 319*(5870), 1687-1688. doi: 10.1126/science.1150952

Hill, N. (1994). *Napoleon Hill's Keys to Success: The 17 Principles of Personal Achievement*. New York: Dutton.

Kiisel, T. (2013). You Are Judged by Your Appearance: Fat people get paid less. Retrieved 23 August 2020, from https://www.forbes.com/sites/tykiisel/2013/03/20/ you-are-judged-by-your-appearance/#54875ec66d50

Kiisel, T. (2013). You Are Judged by Your Appearance: Women who wear makeup make more. Retrieved 23 August 2020, from https:// www.forbes.com/sites/tykiisel/2013/03/20/ you-are-judged-by-your-appearance/#291bf8426d50

Kiisel, T. (2013). You Are Judged by Your Appearance: Workers who work out get paid more. Retrieved 23 August 2020, from https:// www.forbes.com/sites/tykiisel/2013/03/20/ you-are-judged-by-your-appearance/#291bf8426d50

Kruse, K. (2016). The 80/20 Rule and How It Can Change Your Life. Retrieved 23 August 2020, from https://www.forbes.com/sites/ kevinkruse/2016/03/07/80-20-rule/#7361fe903814

Lazar, S. (2018). *How Meditation Changes the Brain* [Video]. Retrieved from https://www.youtube.com/ watch?v=GOIwtTmpc-I

Malkiel, B. (2011). *A Random Walk Down Wall Street: The Time-Tested Strategy for Successful Investing* (10th ed.). New York: W. W. Norton & Company.

Nauert PhD, R. (2018). Doing for Others Also Benefits Health of Altruistic. *Psych Central*. Retrieved from https://psychcentral.com/news/2013/02/06/doing-for-others-also-benefits-health-of-altruistic/51274.html

Oerman, A. (2019). 5 Health Benefits of Red, Red Wine—In Case You Need An(other) Excuse. Retrieved 23 August 2020, from https://www.cosmopolitan.com/health-fitness/a26256554/red-wine-benefits/

Pareto principle. Retrieved 23 August 2020, from https://en.wikipedia.org/wiki/Pareto_principle

Publishing, H. (2010). The health benefits of strong relationships - Harvard Health. Retrieved 23 August 2020, from https://www.health.harvard.edu/newsletter_article/the-health-benefits-of-strong-relationships

Steiner-Adair, C., & Barker, T. (2014). *The Big Disconnect: Protecting Childhood and Family Relationships in the Digital Age*. New York: Harper Paperbacks.

The PEW Charitable Trust. (2015). *The Complex Story of American Debt* (pp. 6-23). The Pew Charitable Trusts. Retrieved from https://www.pewtrusts.org/~/media/assets/2015/07/reach-of-debt-report_artfinal.pdf?la=en

Wilson, C. (2018). Ciara – Level Up Song Lyrics | Genius Lyrics. Retrieved 23 August 2020, from https://genius.com/Ciara-level-up-lyrics

ABOUT THE AUTHOR

I WAS BORN and raised in the city of San Francisco. As a graduate of the Fashion Institute of Design and Merchandising, I am a free, and creative soul. I love nature, volunteering, Bikram yoga, basketball and dressing up.

When I became a first-time mom, I really had no clue. Often as brand-new moms we're just trying to make it. We just Created A Human. That little human used our body as a house for 9 months. Let that sink in....Nothing short of a miracle!

When I first became a new mom, I wished there were an all-encompassing book out there to guide me through the incredible, yet challenging journey called motherhood. After the passing of my Mother, I became the full-time caregiver for my brother who has special needs. With my new found responsibility in addition to becoming a single mom, I needed that book more than ever. Alas, there wasn't one, and I just could not leave parenting to chance. So, I began reading, researching, talking to thriving moms and experts, learning from the successes and pitfalls of moms, including my own experiences.

As time moved along friends and family would constantly ask me, how I do it all? Why do I seem so happy? How do I have time and energy to do the things I love? I wanted to share it all, beyond my friends. Through my education, experiences, and life's lessons, *Single Mom And The City*, was born.

I sincerely hope you enjoyed this book.

xoxo,

Takiyah

Made in the USA
Monee, IL
10 May 2020

As far as friends, I thought about the things in which I found interest. I enjoy having brunch and I love to read. I searched Facebook and found groups for my favorite urban fiction authors and joined them. I became super active in the groups and started attending different author/book events as often as possible.

I also went to eventbrite.com and searched for brunch events that catered to young adults. I strategically place myself in spaces that I can thrive and learn while having fun.

You never really notice how much pain you're withholding, until you start to release it. I hope you are proud of yourself. You've made the decision to change your life. That is a big step and something to be commended. I once heard a pastor say "It isn't the job of the person that hurt you to mend you, that is an inside job." Keep that top of mind as you continue on your journey. It's an everyday action step. You have to put in the work to change your life.

With love,
AKS LOVE

Notes …

Notes …

Notes …

Notes ...

Notes …

Create your plan of action ...

Create your plan of action ...

Create your plan of action ...

Create your plan of action ...

Now write a plan of action. For each change, you will formulate a plan that will help you achieve these.

For example:

Goal #1

Stop gossiping ...

1. Mind my business
2. Do not share information that I obtained in confidence
3. Do not engage in any conversations that even bordered gossiping.

Goal #2

Creating a new style...

1. I started by going to Pinterest and finding pictures of the styles I wanted to achieve. I found clothes, shoes and hairstyles I felt would fit me.
2. I found the stores that sold the things I like that was in my price range.
3. I started a budget and purchased clothing that fit the style I wanted. I am finally able to look at the woman I am in the mirror and love what I see.

Of those things, which can you change?

Review your list. How can you go about achieving what you've written?

What are some things that you dislike about yourself? Can they be "fixed"? Can you learn to love and live with them? As for me, I didn't like the fact that I gossiped, or the way that I dressed. Nor did I like the type of men I attracted, and wanted to expand my friendship circle.

Think about the things you don't like. Write them here...

What qualities do you want to possess? Compose a list that describes how you see yourself as a woman.

anything against her like I did in the past. I value her insight on life; and we are going with flow.

The hardest relationship I had to repair was the one with myself. It required the most work and is ongoing each and every day.

First, I sat down and thought about the type of woman I wanted to be, developed a list of qualities I wanted to possess and wrote out the things I disliked about myself. I decided to work towards making the changes that were within my power and gained acceptance for the rest.

Ways to find a therapist:

- Ask for recommendations from friends. Word of mouth is everything. You can get honest reviews about therapists this way as well.
- Therapyforblackgirls.com allow you to search by city, insurance carrier, and even offers virtual sessions.
- Many employers can make referrals. Contact human resources or you may find the information located in your employee break room (or another centrally located space) on a bulletin board. It will be listed as the employee assistance program (EAP) with a phone number. Through this service you can complete a short survey to be connected with a therapist and may receive between 3-6 free therapy sessions. It is all completely confidential.

Do not allow fear to deter you from seeking therapy, it can be life changing. The good news is, at this point you have already started the work. In your hands right now, is the groundwork for being open with your therapist.

I was once a proud member of the "cut a ish off" club. But as I've grown older and more mature, I do recognize that some relationships deserve a second chance. I took some time to reflect on my relationships and decided which ones I could revive. My relationship with my mom was one, followed by some friendships and most importantly, the relationship I had with myself.

With my mom, we just jumped back into a mother daughter thing. We talk every day and our relationship is easy now because I don't hold

My journey towards restoration has included much therapy. Therapy gets a bad rap because of peoples' lack of understanding of why it is needed. We tend to think that we have to be superwoman and fix everything. I know this because I was one of them. I experienced a wide range of emotions before I decided to go to therapy. I asked myself "Why do I have to pay someone to listen to me?" "Am I that bad off?

It was rough. But I sat and prayed and I asked for specific characteristics in a therapist. I wanted someone who looked like me. I needed a peaceful environment. I wanted someone who I could relate to and who offered engaging conversation, yet provides practical solutions tailored to my situation. I'm proud to say that I found just that.

Therapy is needed even after the release because the effects of the things we've gone through lingers.... they don't just go away overnight. We have to realize that we've been through years and years of traumatic experiences; some we still have yet to identify. Therapy offers a fresh, unbiased eye to the things we've endured.

List some specific qualities you would want a therapist that to possess. Separate the qualities into negotiable vs. non-negotiable traits.

Do you have any reservations about prayer? What are they? Why?

Restoration

After releasing the pain, the next step is restoration.

I started with prayer.

Now we look at prayer as this complicated conversation with God. Trust me it's easier than you think. Praying can be just like talking to one of your friends. I'm all about being open and honest. It's the only way you can heal. Talk to Him and tell him how you feel.

Develop a daily routine; wake up a few minutes early. Find a nice quiet place in your home (closets or bathrooms work great, but you aren't limited to these places.) Turn on some soothing music (I like gospel or the sound of rain) and just let your words flow. You can start off with quick "thank you God for life health and strength" prayers until you get more comfortable.

Think about the things you want to happen in your life. The areas you want to change or expand. Pray and ask God if those things are according to his will for your life and to continue to mold you day by day.

Restoration

The action of returning something to a former owner, place, or condition.

Release

Releasing can happen one of two ways. First, you have to think about both your current and past relationships. Ask yourself are they worthy of either repairing or salvaging?

Once this is determined, you can make a sound decision to have a conversation with the people who have hurt you. Simply give them the letters you've already written pertaining to the situations between you.

It is important to be prepared for the fact that some people will not accept accountability for their actions and will therefore be unwilling to apologize. That's ok. Don't allow them become a roadblock to your journey. You've given situations and people too much of your time already.

The second way to release is to simply walk away. Make the decision that you deserve better; and refuse to tolerate people who don't treat you well. Realize that you deserve to be respected. I know it is no easy feat to walk away from people or situations that are familiar and, in many instances, the only thing you've ever known. But, when you know that you are worth more, you'll see that walking away is the best thing you could've ever done.

Release

Allow or enable to escape from confinement; set free.

Now that was the hard part! You've made it through. Hopefully now that you have reflected and processed those feelings…. you feel better.

There are many things that happen in our lives that causes us pain. For the next few pages, reflect on any other topic that has not been addressed. Write about it. Be open and honest with yourself. If it hurts, acknowledge that fact and write it out.

Write a letter to yourself explaining what prompted you to make unhealthy choices in your past. Grant yourself grace for those decisions and move forward.

Is there anything you've done that you seriously regret? Write about anything you've done that makes you upset with yourself.

When you look in the mirror how do you feel about yourself? Do you love what you see or hate it?

I have always battled with an unhealthy level of self-esteem. When I was in high school, I was diagnosed with anxiety. I often suffered with panic attacks. I later became depressed and hated the choices I made as well as the way they affected me. I began having kids at an early age and I didn't feel as though I could live. My days of feeling depressed far outweighed the happy ones. I suffered for a long time with feelings of regret about things I had done.

I would literally think about each and every situation from my past. I didn't think that I would ever develop a friendship or have the ability to maintain romantic involvement. I believed that the disconnection within my family meant that no one else would want to be with me. While growing up, I was told so many times as a how ugly I was; I literally hated looking in the mirror.

I went many years without looking at myself. I wouldn't even take pictures. My mental state was so disturbed that I truly didn't know who I was. I did any and everything to try to make myself feel better.

I had a promiscuous stage. Having sex just to try to get that feeling of love I desired. That didn't work. I ate and ate and ate until I gained so much weight, I really didn't recognize myself. That didn't work.

I did drugs. I took pill after pill after pill. I stayed high to forget the feelings and thoughts that went on in my head. I took so many pills one night that I just knew I would die. That still didn't work. It wasn't until I had become connected to a pastor and involved at church that I finally felt love and freedom.

Do you have an ex that hurt you? Write to them and provide an explanation about how their actions made you feel.

Do you have an ex that you did wrong? Write a letter explaining your actions, accept accountability and offer an apology.

How would you describe your romantic relationships? Have you been in love? Infatuation? Lust? Were you the player? Did you get played?

Boys … Boys … boys. I've put myself through so much trouble and heartbreak dealing with guys. I split myself with trying to be in love and being a playa. In high school I had a guy, but I was stepping out and dealing with other guys on the side. I would often tell him that when I was done in the streets, he would be the one I'd settle down with. That went on for years, until he got fed up and found someone else that could appreciate him.

One of my last relationships that I call my "karma" really threw me around. I allowed him to use my body, my time and even my money. All in the name of love and friendship. It wasn't even worth it.

Do you have a friend that you think owes you and apology? If you do, write to them and explain how and why their actions hurt you.

Do you have a friend that you think you owe and apology? If you do, write to them explaining your actions, the reasons behind them and accept accountability.

What type of friend are you? Do you encourage your friends often? Do you address disagreements head on to avoid confusion? Or do you let things build up?

A Friend

In the last few years, I have made it my mission to become a better friend. In high school and early adulthood, I was definitely a gossiper. As a result, I got into many fights.

For the most part, I've been fortunate to have the same friends for years. I had a friend in particular, we had a good relationship but there were some things that I just could not stand about her. I made the mistake of never expressing my feelings with her. I would frequently stop talking to her and then a few days or weeks later I would pick back up like everything was all good.

It took me about a year or so of no contact with her for me to fully understand that the way I handled our friendship wasn't always friendly. I reached out and apologized and we are friends again.

If you have a family member that you want to thank for having your back, write to them expressing your gratitude.

If there is one (or more) family member(s) that you had/have an issue with, write to them explaining how the situation has affected you.

Were there any situations between you and a particular family member that shaped your life for the good or bad?

Were you and your family close? Was it guaranteed to be a fun time or a fight when you all came together?

My Family

My relationship with my family has always been difficult. We weren't a distant family, but we weren't close knit. My mom wasn't the most liked among her siblings, so whenever we were in their presence, it was pretty obvious. My family constantly gossiped about each other. It wasn't uncommon for everyone to talk about each other in their faces.

I remember a time when I was about 15 or 16 years old and we had family visiting from out of town. We had a big summer storm in Saint Louis that caused the power to go out. Everyone was at my older sister's house because she had power and it was a safe place for everyone. It was a small two-bedroom apartment and it was about 8 – 10 people there.

There was a disagreement because I was sleeping in a bed and my grandma had to sleep on the couch. The tension was high and she was very upset. There was an exchange of name calling and I was very fed up. My grandma and I got into a physical fight! I'm not proud of that moment, but as a teenager I was frustrated and decided to stand up for myself. My family mistreated me for years; that day I decided to never allow them to mistreat me again.

If you could tell your dad how you feel about your relationship, what would you say?

If your dad was absent, write to him and explain how it felt not having him around. Describe specific things you feel you went through that were an indirect result of his absence.

Describe a situation that caused you to feel distrust towards your dad.

Describe a moment between you and your dad that brought you joy.

What was your relationship like with your dad? Was he your protector?
Was he absent?

Write down what you're feeling ...

My Dad

For the most part my relationship with my dad was pretty good. He disciplined me when I needed it and spoiled me the rest of the time. It wasn't until I was in high school, that I was informed that the person who I had known as my father, wasn't my father.

I was beyond hurt. I felt betrayed and like a part of my life was a lie. I acted out for a long time after I found out. I fought a lot and got involved with guys I had no business being around. Learning that my dad wasn't really my dad, hurt something deep inside of me. I was then forced into the realization that my biological dad hadn't bothered being in my life until years later. The feeling of rejection had been awakened again and was now coupled with confusion.

If you could explain to your mom how you feel overall about your relationship, what would you say?

What was an experience with your mom that brought you happiness?

What was one experience that you felt pushed you and your mom apart?

We are going to start off with a reflection on our feelings towards our mothers. What were your experiences like with your mother?

- Did you argue and fight a lot?
- Did it seem like she just never understood you?
- Was she never around?

Reflection

I didn't have the best relationship with my mom when I was growing up. I longed for her love. Between my siblings and her work schedule, I didn't feel as though I got what I needed from her. I wanted to have that super close "mom is my best friend" relationship. We very rarely did family things. There weren't any birthday celebrations or holiday traditions. We didn't have that connection.

My mom had to work. That was my first experience with feeling rejected. I longed for a love from my mother and it led me down a destructive road. I gave my mom hell. In my mind the attention I received from her, even via punishment, or a fight it was enough attention from her for me.

Reflect

To think deeply or carefully about something.

Introduction

How often do you think about things that you've been through? You wonder why it happened to you? You think about the things you've experienced so much that you become depressed from the hurt and the pain?

You become anxious because you don't know if you'll ever find yourself in that position again. You don't know if you'd ever be able succeed in life. You start questioning your self-worth. All these bad things have happened to me... Am I even worthy of being happy? Being loved? Being successful?

I remember asking myself these very same questions. What is it about me? Why am I always the one who gets my feelings hurt? Why did I have to go through this? I would pray so much because I needed to understand. But even though I prayed, I still dwelled on the things that happened to me for far too long. Many of us are guilty of that very same thing; Dwelling on the past so much that we can't even enjoy our present. This journal will help you reflect on your feelings and release them so you can be on your way to restoring your joy.

I pray that you start this journey with an open heart, an open mind and a willingness to be honest with yourself about how you feel—so you can start living a happier healthy lifestyle.

Published, formatted, and interior design by E.Stones, LLC
www.estonesllc.com

Edited by Kimberli Wilson

ISBN: 978-1-7333291-3-2

Reflect Release Restore

Journal

Angela Burris